How to Get Rid of "it"

Before "it" Gets Rid of You

Healing and Deliverance from Addictions

A Practical Self-Help Guide to Spiritual and Personal Growth

A series of easy spiritual exercises, interactive tools,
And step-by-step instructions to receive
Freedom from bondage
And experience spiritual healing and deliverance

Volume One

ISBN-13: 978-1986164115

ISBN-10: 198616411X

How to Get Rid of "it" Before "it" Gets Rid of You

Healing and Deliverance from Addictions

A Practical Self-Help Guide to Spiritual and Personal Growth

A series of easy spiritual exercises, interactive tools,
And step-by-step instructions to receive
Freedom from bondage
And experience spiritual healing and deliverance

Volume One

Compilations of Works
By
Dr. Paulette Douglas

DEDICATION

**This book is dedicated to my Loving, Supportive, Faithful Husband,
Bishop Robert T. Douglas Sr., PhD**

**For the past 28 years, he has inspired me to be the Women that God has ordained me to be
and to continue to minister to God's people and to make full proof of my ministry**

CONTENT

How to Get Rid of "it", Before "it" Gets Rid of You

PREFACE

How to Get Rid of "it", Before "it" Gets Rid of You is a Deliverance and Spiritual Warfare Manual compiled by Dr. Paulette Douglas which is worth reading and re-reading more than once, to empower the reader when confronting personal crisis and trials. Dr. Paulette Douglas has compiled many practical, spiritual books bringing light to the evil that exists. She brings the deliverance ministry to the forefront, explaining how every believer can counteract evil and the devil. Not many believers understand the concept of the Holy Spirit and that we are all called to fight against the devil, our enemy. Dr. Paulette Douglas presents scriptural background and Bible passages from the old and new testaments, as well as prayers to share with the reader that each of us is called to resist and fight against the devil with the power of the Holy Spirit. Dr. Paulette Douglas refers to this as the deliverance ministry and explains this is one of the privileges all believers have at our disposal.

This background scripture material is necessary as many readers may be unfamiliar with these spiritual concepts. The focus on the book is to be a manual; or one stop guide to show the reader what the bible has to say about deliverance as well as to expose the works and deceptions of the devil as well. The cover itself might seem an actual handbook- yet this book is truly a manual for deliverance. This exhaustive book contains too much information to be digested in a single, quick reading. The words contained are life changing. While some traditional readers and those in organized religion may find this book difficult to believe and a bit theatrical, a close-minded attitude is exactly what the devil wants to operate.

It is important to keep in mind the charismatic background of Dr. Paulette Douglas is based on the belief of the real workings of the Holy Spirit and the literal belief in modern day spiritual gifts such as tongues and healing. Much of the book is an invaluable resource where Dr. Douglas has taken scriptural truths and prayers and relates them to the modern-day believer to use and apply when facing any trial or work from the enemy. The scriptural references will empower any reader with a quick resource of how to respond in faith to any difficulty- large and small. It is a spiritual self-help book in the fact that it will allow the reader the tools to look within himself/her-self and identify any areas or issues where Satan has his foothold. Not only that it tells the reader how to face and address these issues! For those who are at a loss of how to begin to approach their spiritual problems there are a number of sample prayers applicable to any number of situations. The reader will get the impression as if this book was written for his or her own situation. This is a book to meditate on and use- and is not intended to collect dust on a book shelf. There are eleven sequels to this handbook which address many other issues that just might cover your "it".

In this twelve-book series, How to Get Rid of "it" Before "it" gets Rid of You we discuss evil spirits and how they operate:
1. The Apostolic anointing and ministry
2. How demons enter and oppress people
3. Curses and how to deal with them
4. Breaking bondages
5. Casting out spirits
6. Healing the wounded heart

7. Ungodly beliefs
8. Ministering to people
9. House cleansing
10. Discerning of spirits

In this volume we deal with the root causes of the "it' of addictions and How to get rid of the "it" of addictions before it gets rid of you. Addictions are something what plagues many people today, whether addiction to food, sex, drugs, alcohol, smoking, spending, masturbation, porn, etc. Some inexperienced deliverance ministers might go after a spirit of addiction, which may bring freedom, but often, it doesn't bring lasting freedom. Many times, there is a root that needs to be pulled up, alongside casting out any residing spirits that are holding the person in bondage to the addiction. Getting to the root of the addiction is the key to bringing a person lasting genuine freedom. I am going to address the most common roots to addictions, and hopefully give you an idea of how this bondage works so that you can minister lasting freedom to this type of bondage.

INTRODUCTION

"It Is Finished"
The Words of Victory

"When Jesus therefore had received the vinegar, he said, "It is finished.""—John 19:30
Words of triumph. In His words, "My God, my God, why hast thou forsaken me?" we heard the Savior's cry of desolation. In His words, "I thirst" we listened to His cry of lamentation. Now there falls upon our ears His cry of jubilation— "It is finished." From the words of the victim we turn now to the words of the Victor. The Cross of Christ has two great sides to it: it showed the profound depths of His humiliation, but it also marked the goal of the Incarnation, and further, it told the consummation of His mission, and it forms the basis of our salvation.

It is finished." What is found in these three words, "It is finished" is wrapped up the Gospel of God. In these words, contained the ground of the believer's assurance. In those words, is discovered the sum of all joy, and the very spirit of all divine consolation. Every" it" that we could ever encounter in our lives was dealt with on the cross therefore; we have the victory through Jesus Christ over any and every "it".

"It is finished." This was not the despairing cry of a helpless martyr. It was not an expression of satisfaction that the termination of His sufferings was now reached. It was not the last gasp of a worn-out life. No, rather was it the declaration on the part of the divine Redeemer that all for which He came from heaven to earth to do, was now done; that all that was needed to reveal the full character of God had now been accomplished; that all that was required by the Law before sinners could be saved, had now been performed—that the full price of our redemption was now paid.

"It is finished." The great purpose of God in the history of man was now accomplished—from the beginning, God's purpose has always been one and indivisible. It had been declared to men in numerous ways: in symbol and type, by mysterious hints and by plain intimations, through Messianic prediction and through didactic declaration. That purpose of God may be summarized thus: to display His grace in the creating of children in His own image and glory. And at the Cross the foundation was laid which was to make this possible and actual.

"It is finished." What was finished? The answer to this question is a very full one, though many excellent expositors have sought to limit the scope of these words and to confine them strictly to a single application. We are told it was the prophecies concerning the sufferings of Jesus which were finished, and that He referred only to this. It is readily granted that the immediate reference was to the Messianic predictions, yet we think there are good and sufficient reasons for not confining our Lord's words here to them. Yea, to us it seems certain that Christ referred specially to His sacrificial work, for all Scripture concerning His suffering and shame was not yet fulfilled. There remained the dismissal of His spirit into the hands of the Father (Psa 31:5); there remained the "piercing" with the spear (Zec 12:10: and note that the word used in Psalm 22:16 for the piercing of His hands and feet—the act of crucifixion—is a different one); there still remained the preserving of His bones unbroken (Psa 34:20), and the burial in the rich man's grave (Isa 53:9).

"It is finished." What was finished? We answer His sacrificial work. It is true there yet remained the act of death itself, which was necessary for the making of atonement. But, as is so often the case here in John's Gospel wherein our text is found (cf. Joh 12:23, 31; 13:31; 16:5; 17:4), the Lord here speaks of the completion of His work. Moreover, it must be remembered that the three hours darkness was already past, the awful cup had already been drained, His precious blood had already been shed, the outpoured wrath of God had already been endured; and these are the primary elements in the making of propitiation. The sacrificial work of Jesus, then, was completed, excepting only the act of death which followed immediately. But, as we shall see, the completing of the sacrificial work made an end of several things.

"It is finished."
1. Here we see the accomplished fulfillment of all the prophecies which had been written of Him here He should die. This is the immediate thought of the context: "When Jesus therefore had received the vinegar, He said, It is finished" (John 19:30). Centuries beforehand, the prophets of God had described step by step the humiliation and suffering which the coming Savior should undergo. One by one these had been fulfilled, wonderfully fulfilled, fulfilled to the very letter. Had prophecy declared that He should be the "woman's seed" (Gen 3:15), then He was "born of a woman" (Gal 4:4). Had prophecy announced that His mother should be a "virgin" (Isa 7:14), then was it literally fulfilled (Mat 1:18). Had prophecy revealed that He should be of the seed of Abraham (Gen 22:18), then mark its fulfillment (Mat 1:1). Had prophecy made it known that He

Prophecy said that He should be named before He was born (Isa 49:1), then so it came to pass (Luke 1:30-31). Had prophecy foretold that He should be born in Bethlehem of Judea (Mic 5:2), then mark how this very village was His birthplace. Had prophecy forewarned that His birth should entail sorrowing for others (Jer 31:15), then behold its tragic fulfillment (Mat 2:14-18). Had prophecy foreshown that the Messiah should appear before the scepter of tribal ascendancy had departed from Judah (Gen 49:10), then so He did, for though the ten tribes were in captivity, Judah was still in the land at the time of His advent. Had prophecy referred to the flight into Egypt and the subsequent return into Palestine, (Hose 11:1 and cf. Isa 49:3, 6), then so it came to pass (Mat 2:1415).

Prophecy made mention of one going before Christ to make ready His way (Mal 3:1), then see its fulfillment in the person of John the Baptist. Had prophecy made it known that at the Messiah's appearing "the eyes of the blind shall be opened, and the ears of the deaf shall be unstopped, then shall the lame man leap as a hart, and the tongue of the dumb sing" (Isa 35:56), then read through the four Gospels and see how blessedly this proved true. Had prophecy spoken of Him as "poor and needy" (Psa 40:17, see beginning of Psalm), then behold Him not having where to lay His head. Had prophecy intimated that He should speak in "parables" (Psa 78:2), then such was frequently His method of teaching. Had prophecy depicted Him stilling the tempest (Psa 107:29), then this is exactly what He did. Had prophecy heralded His "triumphal entry" into Jerusalem (Zec 9:9), then so it came to pass!

Prophecy announced that His person should be despised (Isa 53:3), that He should be rejected by the Jews (Isa 8:14), that He should be "hated without a cause" (Psa 69:4), then sad to say, such was precisely the case. Had prophecy painted the whole picture of His degradation and crucifixion, then was it vividly reproduced. There had been the betrayal by a familiar friend, the forsaking by His disciples, the being led to the slaughter, the being taken to judgment, the appearing of false witnesses against Him, the refusal on His part to make defense, the establishing of His innocence, the unjust condemnation, the sentence of capital punishment passed upon Him, the literal piercing of His hands and feet, the being numbered with transgressors, the mockery of the crowd, the casting lots for His garments—all predicted centuries beforehand, and all fulfilled to the very letter. The last prophecy of all which remained here He committed His Spirit into the hands of His Father, had now been fulfilled. He cried "I thirst," and after the tendering of the vinegar and gall, all was now "accomplished"; and as the Lord Jesus reviewed the entire scope of the prophetic Word and saw its full realization, He cried,

"It is finished"!
It only remains for us to point out that as there was a complete set of prophecies which had to do with the first advent of Jesus, so also is there a complete set of prophecies which have to do with His second advent—the latter as definite, as personal, and as comprehensive in their scope as the former. As then we see the actual fulfillment of those which had to do with His first coming to the earth, we may look forward with absolute confidence and assurance to the fulfillment of those which have to do with His second coming. And, as we have seen that the former set of prophecies were fulfilled literally and personally, so also must we expect the latter set to be. To grant the literal fulfillment of the former, and then to seek to spiritualize and symbolize the latter, is not only grossly inconsistent and illogical, but is highly injurious to us and deeply dishonoring to God and to His Word.

"It is finished."
2. Here we see the completion of His sufferings. But what tongue or pen can describe the sufferings of Jesus? The anguish, physical, mental, and spiritual, which He endured! Appropriately was He designated "the man of sorrows": suffering at the hands of men, at the hands of Satan, and at the hands of God. Pain inflicted upon Him by enemies and friends alike. From the beginning He walked the shadows which the Cross cast His path. "I am afflicted and ready to die from my youth up" (Psa 88:15). What a light this throws on His earlier years! Who can say how much is contained in those words? For us, an impenetrable veil is cast over the future; none of us knows what a day may bring forth.

But Jesus knew the end from the beginning! One has only to read through the Gospels to learn how the awful Cross was ever before Him. At the marriage-feast of Cana, where all was gladness and merriment, He makes solemn reference to "his hour" not yet come. When Nicodemus interviewed Him at night, the Savior referred to the "lifting up of the Son of man." When James and John came to request from Him the two places of honor in His coming kingdom, He made mention of the "cup" which He had to drink, and of the "baptism" wherewith He must be baptized. When Peter confessed that He was the Christ, the Son of the living God, He turned to His disciples and began to show unto them "how that he must go unto Jerusalem, and suffer many things of the elders and chief priests and scribes, and be killed, and be raised again the third day" (Mat 16:21). When Moses and Elijah stood with Him on the Mount of Transfiguration, it was to speak of "his decease which he should accomplish at Jerusalem" (Luke 9:31).

If it is true we are quite unable to estimate the sufferings of Christ due to the anticipation of the Cross, still less can we fathom the dread reality itself. The physical sufferings were excruciating, but even this was as nothing compared with His anguish of soul. To a consideration of these sufferings we have already devoted several paragraphs in previous chapters, yet we make no apology in turning to them again. We cannot contemplate too often what Jesus endured to secure our salvation. The better we are acquainted with His sufferings, and the more frequently we meditate thereon, the warmer will be our love and the deeper our gratitude.
At last the closing hours have come. There had been the terrible experience in Gethsemane followed by the appearing before Caiaphas, before Pilate, before Herod, and back again before Pilate. There had been the scourging and mocking by the brutal soldiers; the journey to Calvary; the fastening of His hands and feet to the cruel tree. There had been the reviling of the priests, the crowd, and the two thieves crucified with Him.

There had been the awful cloud that hid from the Father's face, which wrung from Him the bitter cry, "My God, my God, why hast thou forsaken me?" There had been the parched lips which drew from Him the exclamation "I thirst." There had been the fearful conflict with the power of darkness as the serpent "bruised" His heel. But now the suffering is ended. The Lord has bruised Him; man, and Devil have done their worst. The cup has been drained. The awful storm of God's wrath has spent itself. The darkness is ended. The sword of divine justice is done. The wages of sin have been paid. The prophecies of His sufferings are all fulfilled. The Cross has been "endured." Divine holiness has been fully satisfied (Isa 53:11). With a cry of triumph—a loud cry, a cry which reverberated throughout the entire universe—Jesus exclaims, "It is finished." The shame, the suffering and agony, are past. Never again shall He experience pain. Never again shall He endure the contradiction of sinners against Himself. Never again shall He be in the hands of Satan. Never again shall the light of God's countenance be hidden from Him. Blessed be God, all that is finished! "It is finished."

Jesus is concerned in the work of Redemption: He was the One who came here to die for sinners. He is the One who now gives spiritual illumination and understanding, and guides into the truth. Before the Lord Jesus came to this earth, a definite work was committed to Him. In the volume of the book it was written of Him, and He came to do the recorded will of God. Even as a boy of twelve the "Father's business" was before His heart and occupied His attention. Again, in John 5:36 we find Him saying, "But I have greater witness than that of John: for the works which the Father hath given me to finish, the same works that I do." And on the last night before His death, in that wonderful high priestly prayer, we find Him saying, "I have glorified thee on the earth: I have finished the work which thou gavest me to do" (John 17:4).

The mission upon which God had sent His Son into the world was now accomplished. It was not actually finished till He breathed His last, but death was only an instant ahead, and in anticipation of it He cries "It is finished." The demanding work is done. The divinely-given task is performed. A work more honorable and momentous than ever entrusted to man or angels, has been completed. That for which He had left heaven's glory that for which He had taken upon Him the form of a servant, that for which He had remained upon earth for thirty-three years to do, was now consummated. Nothing remained to be added. The goal of the Incarnation is reached. With what joyous triumph must He here have viewed the costly work which, committed to Him, had now been perfected!

"It is finished." The mission upon which God had sent His Son into the world was accomplished. That which had been eternally purposed had come to pass. The plan of God had been fully carried out.

Because He is the Most High, God's will, cannot be thwarted. Because He is supreme, God's counsel must stand. Because He is almighty, God's purpose cannot be overthrown.
"But he is in one mind, and who can turn him? And what his soul desireth, even that he doeth" (Job 23:13). "I know that thou canst do everything, and that no thought can be withholding from thee" (Job 42:2). "But our God is in the heavens: He hath done whatsoever he hath pleased" (Psa 115:3). "There is no wisdom nor understanding nor counsel against the Lord" (Pro 21:30). "For the Lord of hosts hath purposed, and who shall disannul it? And His hand is stretched out, and who shall turn it back?" (Isa 14:27). "Remember the former things of old: for I am God, and there is none else; I am God, and there is none like me: Declaring the end from the beginning, and from ancient times the things that are not yet done, saying, My counsel shall stand, and I will do all my pleasure" (Isa 46:9-10). "And all the inhabitants of the earth are reputed as nothing: and he doeth according to his will in the army of heaven, and among the inhabitants of the earth: and none can stay his hand, or say unto him, What doest thou?" (Dan 4:35). And, in the triumphant cry of the Jesus— "It is finished"—we have a prophecy and pledge of the ultimate carrying out of God's plan completely. At the end of time, when everything is wound up, and God's purpose has been fully consummated, when everything has been done which He before determined should be done, then shall it be said again, "It is finished."

"It is finished."
4. Here we see the accomplishment of the Atonement. Above we have spoken of Christ reaching the goal of the Incarnation, and of the consummation of His mission to the earth; what that goal and mission was, the Scriptures plainly reveal. The Son of Man came here "to seek and to save that which was lost" (Luke 19:10). Christ Jesus came into the world "to save sinners" (1Ti 1:15). God sent forth His Son, born of a woman, "to redeem them that were under the law" (Gal 4:5). He was manifested "to take away our sins" (1Jo 3:5). And all this involved the Cross. The "lost" which He came to seek could only be found there—in the place of death and under the condemnation of God. Sinners could be "saved" only by One taking their place and bearing their iniquities. They who were under the Law could be "redeemed" only by Another fulfilling its requirements and suffering its curse. Our sins could be "taken away" only by their being blotted out by the precious blood of Christ. The demands of justice must be met; the requirements of God's holiness must be satisfied; the awful debt we incurred must be paid. And on the Cross, this was done; done by none less than the Son of God; done perfectly; done once for all.

"It is finished."
That to which so many types looked forward, was now accomplished. A covering from sin and its shame, typified by the coats of skin with which the Lord God clothed our first parents, was now provided. The more excellent sacrifice, typified by Abel's lamb, had now been offered. A shelter from the storm of divine judgment, typified by the Ark of Noah, was now furnished. The only-begotten and well-beloved Son, typified by Abraham's offering up of Isaac, had already been placed upon the altar. A protection from the avenging angel, typified by the shed blood of the Passover-lamb, was now supplied. A cure from the serpent's bite, typified by the serpent of

brass upon the pole, was now made ready for sinners. The providing of a life-giving fountain, typified by Moses striking the rock, was now affected.

"It is finished." The Greek word here, teleo, is translated variously in the New Testament. A glance at some of the different renderings in other passages will enable us to discern the fullness and finality of the term used by Jesus. In Matthew 11:1, teleo is rendered as follows, "When Jesus had made an end of commanding his twelve disciples, he departed thence." In Matthew 17:24 it is rendered, "They that received tribute money came to Peter, and said, Doth not your master pay tribute?" In Luke 2:39, it is rendered, "And when they had performed all things according to the Law of the Lord, they returned into Galilee." In Luke 18:31, it is rendered, "All things that are written by the prophets concerning the Son shall be accomplished."

"It is finished." He cried: it is "made an end of"; it is "paid"; it is "performed"; it is "accomplished." What was made an end of? —our sins and their guilt. What was "paid?"—the price of our redemption. What was "performed?"—the utmost requirements of the Law. What was "accomplished?"—the work which the Father had given Him to do. What was "finished?"—the making of atonement. God has furnished at least four proofs that Christ did finish the work which was given Him to do. First, in the rending of the veil, which showed that the way to God was now open. Second, in the raising of Christ from the dead, which evidenced that God had accepted His sacrifice. Third, the exaltation of Christ to His own right hand, which demonstrated the value of Christ's work and the Father's delight in His person. Fourth, the sending to earth of the Holy Spirit to apply the virtues and benefits of Christ's atoning death.

"It is finished." What was "finished?"—the work of atonement. What is the value of that to us? This: to the sinner, it is a message of glad tidings. All that a Holy God requires has been done. Nothing is left for the sinner to add. No works from us are demanded as the price of our salvation. All that is necessary for the sinner is to rest now by faith upon what Christ did. "The gift of God is eternal life through Jesus Christ our Lord" (Rom 6:23). To the believer, the knowledge that the atoning work of Christ is finished brings a sweet relief over against all the defects and imperfections of his services. There is nothing "finished" that we do: all our duties are imperfect. There is much of sin and vanity in the very best of our efforts, but the grand relief is that we are "complete" in Christ (Col 2:10)! Christ and His finished work are the ground of all our hopes. "It is finished."

5. Here we see the end of our sins. The sins of the believer, all of them, were transferred to the Jesus. As the Scripture says, "The Lord hath laid on him the iniquities of us all" (Isa 53:6). If then God laid my iniquities on Christ, they are no longer on me. Sin there is in me, for the old Adamic nature remains in the believer till death or till Christ's return, should He come before I die; but there is no sin on me. This distinction between sin in and sin on, is a vital one, and there should be little difficulty in apprehending it. If I were to say the judge passed sentence on a criminal, and that he is now under sentence of death, everyone would understand what I meant. In like manner, everyone out of Christ has the sentence of God's condemnation resting upon him. But when a sinner believes in the Lord Jesus, and receives Him as his Lord and Master, obey the salvation message according to (Acts 2:38-39) he is no longer "under condemnation"— sin is no longer on him, that is, the guilt, the condemnation, the penalty of sin, is no longer upon him. And why? Because Christ bore our sins in His own body on the tree (1Pe 2:24)—the guilt,

condemnation, and penalty of our sins, was transferred to our substitute. Hence, because my sins were transferred to Christ, they are no more upon me.

This precious truth was strikingly illustrated in Old Testament times regarding Israel's annual Day of Atonement. On that day, Aaron, the high priest (a type of Christ), made satisfaction to God for the sins which Israel had committed during the previous year. The way this was done is described in Leviticus 16. Two goats were taken and presented before the Lord at the door of the tabernacle: this was before anything was done with them: it represented Christ being sent and presenting Himself, offering to come into this world and be the Savior of sinners. One of the goats was then taken and killed, and its blood was carried into the tabernacle, within the veil, into the Holy of Holies, and there it was sprinkled before and upon the mercy seat—foreshadowing Christ offering Himself as a sacrifice, to meet the demands of His justice and satisfy the requirements of His holiness.

Then we read that Aaron came out of the tabernacle and laid both his hands upon the head of the second (living) goat— signifying an act of identification by which Aaron is the representative of the whole nation, identified the people with it, acknowledging that its doom was what their sins merited, and which, today, corresponds with the hands of faith laying hold of Christ and identifying ourselves with Him in His Death. Having laid his hands on the head of the live goat, Aaron now confessed over him "all the iniquities of the children of Israel, and all their transgressions in all their sins, putting them upon the head of the goat" (Lev 16:21). Thus, were Israel's sins transferred to their substitute. Finally, we are told, "And the goat shall bear upon him all their iniquities unto a land not inhabited: and he shall let go the goat in the wilderness" (Lev 16:22). The goat bearing Israel's sins, was taken unto an uninhabited wilderness, and the people of God saw him and their sins no more! In type this was Christ taking our sins into that desolate land where God was not and there making an end of them. The Cross of Christ then is the grave of our sins!

"It is finished."
6. Here we see the fulfillment of the Law's requirements. "The law is holy, and the commandment holy, and just and good" (Rom 7:12). How could it be anything less when Jehovah Himself had framed and given it! The fault lay not in the Law but in man who, being depraved and sinful, could not keep it. Yet that Law must be kept, and kept by a man, so that the Law might be honored and magnified, and its giver vindicated. Therefore, we read, "For what the law could not do, in that it was weak through the flesh, God sending his own Son, in the likeness of sinful flesh, and for sin, condemned sin in the flesh: that the righteousness of the law might be fulfilled in [not by] us, who walk not after flesh, but after the Spirit" (Rom 8:3-4). The "weakness" here is that of fallen man. The sending forth of God's Son in the likeness of sin's flesh (Greek) refers to the Incarnation: as we read in another Scripture, "God sent forth his Son, born of a woman, born under the law, that he might redeem them that were under the law" (Gal 4:4-5 RV). Yes, the Jesus was born "under the law," born under it that He might keep it perfectly in thought, word, and deed. "Think not that I am come to destroy the law, or the prophets: I am not come to destroy, but to fulfill" (Mat 5:17); such was His claim.

But not only did Jesus keep the precepts of the Law, He also suffered its penalty and endured its curse. We had broken it, and taking our place, He must receive its just sentence. Having received its penalty and endured its curse, the demands of the Law are fully met, and justice is satisfied. Therefore, is it written of believers, "Christ hath redeemed us from the curse of the law, being made a curse for us" (Gal 3:13). And again, "For Christ is the end of the law for righteousness to everyone that believeth" (Rom 10:4). And yet again, "For ye are not under the law, but under grace" (Rom 6:14). "It is finished." "Free from the Law, Jesus hath bled, and there is remission, cursed by the law and bruised by the fall, Grace hath redeemed us once for all."

7. Here we see the destruction of Satan's power. See it by faith. The Cross sounded the death of the devil's power. To human appearances it looked like the moment of his greatest triumph, yet, it was the hour of his ultimate defeat. In view of the Cross Jesus declared, "Now is the judgment of this world: now shall the prince of this world be cast out" (Joh 12:31). It is true that Satan has not yet been chained and cast into the bottomless pit, nevertheless, sentence has been passed (though not yet executed); his doom is certain; and his power is already broken so far as believers are concerned.

For the Christian, the devil is a vanquished foe. He was defeated by Christ at the Cross— "that through death he might destroy him that had the power of death, that is, the devil" (Hebrew 2:14). Believers have already been "delivered from the power of darkness" and translated into the kingdom of God's dear Son (Col 1:13). Satan, then, should be treated as a defeated enemy. No longer has he any legitimate claim upon us. Once we were his lawful "captives"; but now God worketh in us both to will and to do of His good pleasure. All that we now must do is to "resist the devil," and the promise is, "he will flee from you" (James 4:7).

"It is finished." Here was the triumphant answer to the rage of man and the enmity of Satan. It tells of the perfect work which meets sin in the place of judgment. All was completed just as God would have it, just as the prophets had foretold, just as the Old Testament ceremonial had foreshadowed, just as divine holiness demanded, and just as sinners needed. How strikingly appropriate is this sixth Cross-utterance of Jesus found in John's Gospel—the Gospel which displays the glory of Christ's deity! He seals it with His own words, attesting it is complete, and giving it the all-sufficient sanction of His own approval. Jesus says, "It is finished"—who then dare doubt or question it.

"It is finished." Reader, do you believe it? or, are you trying to add something of your own to the finished work of Christ to secure the favor of God? All you must do is to accept the pardon which He purchased. God is satisfied with His work on the cross, why are not you? Sinner, the moment you believe Jesus' testimony that it is finished, that moment every sin you have committed is blotted out, and you stand accepted in Christ! O would you not like to possess the assurance that there is nothing between your soul and God? Would you not like to know that every sin had been atoned for and put away? Then believe what God's Word says about Christ's death. Rest not on your feelings and experiences but on the written Word. There is only one way of finding peace, deliverance, wholeness, salvation, victory over the "it" and that is through faith in the shed blood of Jesus the of Lamb God. It is time to "Get Rid of "it", Before "it" Gets Rid of You".

"It is finished." Do you really believe it? Or, are you endeavoring to add something of your own to it and thus merit the favor of God? By continuing to hold on and struggle, seeking other sources to deal with the "it" in your life, you are nullifying the finished work of Christ by your own miserable additions to it!". The Gospel of God's grace, and the finished work of Christ is sufficient for our souls to rest upon. In the pages of this book, God uses forceful object lessons and His Word to show you, "How to Get Rid of "it", before "it" Gets Rid of You". It is a grave mistake not to embrace the Word of God, and cast yourself by faith upon what Christ had done for you.

Victory was given to us by way of the cross. Whatever your "it" or "its" might be, "it" has come to kill, steal and destroy you. Make a conscious effort to explore this information given in this book and expose the enemy of your soul. Let's "Get Rid of "it". After all, "It is Finished"

CHAPTER ONE

What is "it"?

We are all created with a basic need to be loved. God created us to both give and receive love, but though damaged emotions, our capacity to receive love can be dramatically hindered. Ignorance of God's love will also hinder us from receiving the great and glorious love that He has for us. **The root of most "its" is a lack of love being received by that person.** Many of us have been damaged emotionally by rejection, abandonment, abuse, etc., and thereby our capacity to receive love has been reduced. **Only an emotionally healthy person is capable of both giving and receiving love as God intended.**

Self-worth issues can hinder love

Self-worth issues are rooted in believing that we are not worthy or deserve to be loved. When we believe that we are unlovable, we will unconsciously reject any love that comes our way. We won't believe the love, because we believe in our hearts that we are not worthy. **Self-worth issues are all rooted in our failing to see who we really are in Christ.**

If you walked into a gallery of world-class art, and pointed to a painting, saying, "That is the ugliest thing I've ever seen! Who painted that??" Now let's say the artist was standing right next to you. How do you think that would make him feel? Do you realize we are the artwork of God, a special painting crafted together by the master painter? Do you think it brings Him honor when we look down on ourselves? **We need to stop putting down what God has made.**

Many times, we have self-unforgiveness issues because we blame ourselves for something, or we've done something we deeply regret, and we simply cannot let it go. We need to realize that Jesus has forgiven us of all our failures, and we need to start seeing ourselves as forgiven. Otherwise, we're denying the work of Christ in our life! **If God forgave you, and you're still beating yourself up, then you don't really believe what Jesus did for you.** It's that simple!

Just as we must forgive others (see Matthew 18:21-35), we need to forgive ourselves just the same. Self-hate has been known to be the root behind diseases such as lupus and Crohn's disease, as well as other auto-immune diseases. We need to stop holding ourselves accountable for that which Jesus has set us free from.

If we want to be in faith, we need to BELIEVE what Jesus did for us, and part of that believing is seeing ourselves as forgiven and clothed with the righteousness of God, which is upon all who believe in the finished work of Christ. Without faith, it is impossible to please God (see Hebrews 11:6), so if you want to please God, start taking the finished work of the cross seriously, and begin to see yourself as forgiven, washed clean, and clothed in the righteousness of God. For the righteousness (right standing with God) is upon all who believe:

> *"Even the righteousness of God which is by faith of Jesus Christ unto all and upon all them that believe..." (Romans 3:22 KJV)*

Unforgiveness is rooted in a lack of realization of how much God has forgiven us, and therefore we're not thankful for the steep and terrible price that Jesus paid for our own failures. Therefore, it is so important to mediate on what Jesus did for us, until it transforms our heart. The message of Jesus' work for us is what causes faith to arise in our hearts and transforms us from the inside out (read Romans 10:8-17).

Learning to see yourself as God sees you, and forgive yourself because you want to please God and be in faith and be thankful for what Jesus did for you, is the biggest step in overcoming self-worth issues. Of course, there are spirits that may need to be driven out as well, such as self-hate, guilt, condemnation, etc.

Receiving the love God has for us

When it comes to God's love for us, that's obvious, considering how He loves even the sinner so much that Jesus came to die for them. Anybody who knows the message of the cross, has some knowledge of God's love for us. However, many times, we blame God for our problems, and so we don't believe the love that He has for us. Not only do we blame Him for our problems, many times we think that God gave us the sickness or problem in our life to teach us something. Nothing could be further from the truth! Jesus tells us clearly who came to kill, steal, and destroy, and who came so that we could have life and have it in abundance.

> *"The thief cometh not, but for to steal, and to kill, and to destroy: I am come that they might have life, and that they might have it more abundantly." (John 10:10 KJV)*

If we are going to receive the love that God has for us, we need to get our thinking straightened out. He's not the one behind our problems, but rather Jesus paid the full price so that we can be forgiven all our sins, both physically and emotionally healed, and blessed.

> *"When the even was come, they brought unto him many that were possessed with devils: and he cast out the spirits with his word, and healed all that were sick: That it might be fulfilled which was spoken by Esaias the prophet, saying, Himself took our infirmities, and bare our sicknesses." (Matthew 8:16-17 KJV)*

Look at how good God's heart is toward mankind! Not only did Jesus heal them, but He proved the blessings of the covenant we have with Him today concerning our healing and deliverance. Isn't He good toward us? **The reason why things happen to us, is because we live in a fallen world that is under the control of the evil one.** <u>It's not God's fault. He loves you. Jesus died for you.</u>

Settling the fact that God loves you and is good toward you is crucial to restoring your God-given capacity to receive His love. If you can't receive His love, then you need to stop and ask yourself four questions:

1. Am I blaming God for anything bad that happened to me?

2. Have I been emotionally wounded in such a way that it is hindering my ability to freely receive love as God intended me to?

3. Do I have knowledge and revelation of how much God loves me? Do I have a solid Biblical understanding of how I am loved with the same kind of love that the Father has for Jesus?

4. Is there a self-worth issue that makes me feel unworthy to be loved?

Settling these issues lays a foundation for breaking free from the power of the "IT". You must repair the damage and faulty thinking which hinders your ability to receive the love that God has for you.

How do you know if you are receiving God's love or if it's hindered? **If you are not passionate about Jesus, then somewhere your ability to receive His love is hindered.**

If you are living a life without receiving God's love in your heart daily, you are missing out on the most fulfilling life you can have here on this earth. To know God's love, which surpasses all understanding (see Philippians 4:7), dispels all our fears and gives us a sense of peace and joy that we could never otherwise know.

"And we have known and believed the love that God hath to us. God is love; and he that dwelleth in love dwelleth in God, and God in him. Herein is our love made perfect, that we may have boldness in the day of judgment: because as he is, so are we in this world. <u>There is no fear in love; but perfect love casteth out fear</u>: because fear hath torment. <u>He that feareth is not made perfect in love.</u>" (1 John 4:16-18 KJV)

What exactly is "it"?

An "it" is formed when we try to use something other than God, to meet our need to be loved. When our ability to receive God's love into our hearts is hindered, we will feel like something is missing, and seek to fill that void with something else. When that thing, whatever it might be, fills that void, we grow to love "it" because it's meeting a need. Over time, we establish a relationship with that thing, and when it comes time to depart, it's like breaking up a relationship. That's why the "it" is so destructive; we've relied on that thing to meet a need and we've established a relationship with it. Now when it's time to break up the love, it isn't so easy to say goodbye.

One widespread problem that we see when we try to deal with "it", is where we give up one "it" successfully, only to find yourself with another "it". We might quit drinking only to start overeating, for example. We might think we're finding victory, but all we're really doing is trading one "it" for another "it". This is because something must fill the love-void in our hearts, and if it's not one thing, it will be another.

What about cutting or self-harm?

Cutting or self-mutation is a special type of "it", where there's a need to either release pain in a person's heart or the person believes that they deserve to be punished for their failures. In these cases, the person certainly has an issue receiving the love that God has for them but there's another type of root that needs to be addressed as well. There's emotional pain or guilt that the person is dealing with that needs to be resolved. Finding out what happened and receiving Christ's truth concerning those areas is important for their healing. Any bondage involving guilt will need to be resolved through realizing and accepting the work of Christ on the cross for that person and they will likely need spirits of guilt, condemnation, self-hate, etc. driven out in Jesus' name. Again, getting the person to see them self for who they really are in Christ, forgiven, loved, and blessed, is crucial to lasting freedom from self-hate issues.

See yourself as lovable!

The key in uprooting most "its" is to deal with the underlying issues which are limiting their capacity to freely receive love from God and others, along with dealing with any self-worth issues by establishing an understanding of your true identity in Christ. **Coming to a place where you believe you are lovable is key to receiving love in general**, so dealing with self-worth issues is an important key to breaking down the walls which keep us from feeling loved. The only way to obtain a true sense of worth and value is to get a revelation of how much you are loved by God, who sent His son Jesus to die for you.

Discovering the root

To discover the root of your "it", you need to get real honest with yourself. Many times, we are in denial about the pain we are feeling. Figuring out what is the root of a bondage is all about asking the right questions, and that is especially important when it comes to uprooting an "it". Why don't we feel loved? Do we feel unlovable? (Let's stop right there; if we feel unlovable, then you've just discovered a self-worth issue that will need to be addressed.) Are you passionate about Jesus? If not, then something in hindering you from realizing how much you are loved by Him who died for you. Do you see yourself as forgiven and loved by the God because of what He did for you?

As you discover emotional wounds, you'll need to forgive (others, yourself, and God) and invite Jesus to come and heal the damage in your heart. If you don't realize how much God loves you, then you'll need to spend some time learning about what Jesus did for you on the cross, and what a terrible price He paid because He loved you so very much. Often breaking out of an "it" is a combination of emotional healing, learning about who you are in Christ, forgiving (yourself, others, and God), overcoming self-worth issues by changing how you see yourself (in light of how God sees and loves you), and casting out any spirits that came in and are enforcing the destructive behavior. Spirits behind guilt, condemnation, etc. also need to be driven out, as they seek to keep us from fully seeing what Jesus did for us on the cross.

Dealing with the issues underlying an "it" is key to uprooting it permanently. If you want lasting freedom and wholeness in this area of your life, you will have to deal with the issues that have limited your capacity to receive love, especially the love that God has for you.

CHAPTER TWO

**The "it" of Additions
(Drug, Alcohol, Gambling, Sexual)**

DEFINITION: People with addictions have lost control over what they think, what they do, or what they ingest into their bodies. The term "addiction" can be applied to harmful substances such as drugs, alcohol, and cigarettes. It can also be applied to harmful behaviors such as compulsive gambling, sex, or mutilating your own body. People can also develop addictions to things that in themselves are not harmful--such as food, hobbies, sports, etc.--but that are addictions when used in uncontrolled excesses.

FACTS ABOUT ADDICTION:

So, you think you aren't addicted? If you answer yes to any of the following questions, you need help:

-Are you using drugs other than those required and prescribed for medical reasons?
-Can you get through the week without using alcohol or drugs?
-Has your drug/alcohol abuse interfered with relationships with your parents, children, spouse, relatives, or friends?
-Has your drug/alcohol use caused you to miss days at work or school?
-Have you been dismissed from school, a job, school, or other positions due to drug/alcohol use?
-Have you had a fight when under the influence of alcohol or a drug?
-Have you done anything illegal to obtain alcohol or drugs?
-Have you been arrested for possession of illegal drugs?
-Have you been arrested for driving under the influence of drugs or alcohol?
-Have you had medical problems (like memory loss, hepatitis, convulsions, blackouts, flashbacks etc.) because of using drugs or alcohol?
-Do you feel sick when you try to stop using drugs or alcohol?

You are a slave to whatever controls you. *"A man is a slave to whatever has mastered him" (2 Peter 2:19).*

You cannot please God if you are controlled by addictions. *"Those controlled by the sinful nature cannot please God. You, however, are controlled not by the sinful nature but by the Spirit, if the Spirit of God lives in you" (Romans 8:8-9).*

Anything that harms your body spiritually, mentally, or physically is sin. The Bible declares: *"Don't you know that you yourselves are God's temple and that God's Spirit lives in you? If anyone destroys God's temple, God will destroy him; for God's temple is sacred, and you are that temple" (1 Corinthians 3:16-17)* . Your body is a temple and you should treat it as a sanctuary.

Addictions cause you to lose control. When you are under the influence of an addiction, you lose control of your will, your body, and your mental processes. If you are not in control and God is not in control, guess who is? Your enemy, Satan.

Drugs are related to sorcery. Revelation 18:23 speaks of the "sorceries" of evil men. The Greek word for sorceries is "pharmakeia", meaning "enchantment with drugs". Revelation 9:21 indicates that those that do not repent of their "sorceries" (enchantment with drugs) cannot enter the Kingdom of God.

Legitimate drugs, when not abused, are not sinful. Every good gift comes from God, and legitimate medications are gifts that help restore health and alleviate pain.

There are many kinds of addictions. A person can be addicted to food, drugs, alcohol, gambling, sex, or pornography. One may also be addicted to an activity that is not wrong, but because of overindulgence in it becomes wrong.

God wants you free from all addictions. *"It is for freedom that Christ has set us free. Stand firm, then, and do not let yourselves be burdened again by a yoke of slavery" (Galatians 5:1).*

DEALING WITH ADDICTION:

Admit that your addiction is sin. If you refuse to admit your addiction, you will be unable to deal with it. *"He who conceals his sins does not prosper, but whoever confesses and renounces them finds mercy" (Proverbs 28:13).*

Cut the root, kill the fruit. Addiction is a surface manifestation of a deeper need or problem in your life. Think about why you take drugs, drink, smoke, gamble, etc.? Do you feel better about yourself when you do it? Do you do it to try to escape heartache and difficulties in your life? Whether it be heartache, difficulties, or negative emotions, etc., cut the root that is supporting your habit and you will kill the fruit--the addiction itself.

Ask God for deliverance. Pray not only about your addiction, but the root causes behind it-- your hurt, pain, rejection issues, etc. Rebuke any generational spirits that would foster addictions. Bind the spirit of addiction from operating in your life: *"I tell you the truth, whatever you bind on earth will be bound in heaven, and whatever you loose on earth will be loosed in heaven" (Matthew 18:18).* Renew your mind by the Word, prayer, and meditation.

Seek biblical rehabilitation. If you need assistance in dealing with your addiction, find a biblical rehabilitation center or program. The Salvation Army, Teen Challenge, Dream Centers, and Celebrate Recovery are excellent biblically-based programs.

Resist the devil. *"Submit yourselves, then, to God. Resist the devil, and he will flee from you. Come near to God and he will come near to you..." (James 4:7-8a).* You resist the devil and his temptations by prayer and the Word of God which enables you to draw near to God. You are not resisting the devil when you have cigarettes or drugs in your pocket just "in case it doesn't work" and you need them. Use your access to God to secure help in time of need (Hebrews 4:15-16).

Change your lifestyle. Do not hang out with people who use drugs or alcohol. Do not frequent parties or places where drugs or alcohol are used, or gambling is done. Do not watch television programs that promote drugs, alcohol, gambling, etc. through either the screenplay or advertising. Do not return to the bondage of addiction (Galatians 5:1).

Form a support network. Form a personal support network of people who have successfully recovered from addictions and can help you do the same. Celebrate Recovery and Teen Challenge provide excellent Christian support networks for addictions.

Know that you will be tempted. Temptation is common when overcoming an addiction, but you can overcome it in the power of the Lord. When you are tempted by the enemy to engage in that habit again remember that... *"No temptation has seized you except what is common to man. And God is faithful; he will not let you be tempted beyond what you can bear. But when you are tempted, he will also provide a way out so that you can stand up under it"* (1 Corinthians 10:13). There is always a way out. Take it!

Remember that you never fail until you quit trying. If you return to your addiction, do not give up in defeat. Ask God to forgive you and strengthen you to take control over the addiction, then begin again. Rather than condemning yourself, think about ways you can respond better next time you are tempted.

WHAT GOD'S WORD SAYS ABOUT ADDICTION:

I tell you the truth, everyone who sins is a slave to sin. Now a slave has no permanent place in the family, but a son belongs to it forever. (John 8:34-35)

For I have the desire to do what is good, but I cannot carry it out. (Romans 7:18)

For what I do is not the good I want to do; no, the evil I do not want to do--this I keep doing... What a wretched man I am! Who will rescue me from this body of death? Thanks be to God through Jesus Christ our Lord! (Romans 7:19 and 24-25)

Those controlled by the sinful nature cannot please God. You, however, are controlled not by the sinful nature but by the Spirit, if the Spirit of God lives in you. (Romans 8:8-9)

For if you live according to the sinful nature, you will die; but if by the Spirit you put to death the misdeeds of the body, you will live, because those who are led by the Spirit of God are sons of God. (Romans 8:13-14)

Clothe yourselves with the Lord Jesus Christ, and do not think about how to gratify the desires of the sinful nature. (Romans 13:14)

Don't you know that you yourselves are God's temple and that God's Spirit lives in you? If anyone destroys God's temple, God will destroy him; for God's temple is sacred, and you are that temple. (1 Corinthians 3:16-17)

Everything is permissible for me-but not everything is beneficial. Everything is permissible for me-but I will not be mastered by anything. (1 Corinthians 6:12)

Do you not know that your body is a temple of the Holy Spirit, who is in you, whom you have received from God? You are not your own; you were bought at a price. Therefore honor God with your body. (1 Corinthians 6:19-20)

So whether you eat or drink or whatever you do, do it all for the glory of God. (1 Corinthians 10:31)

For we are the temple of the living God. (2 Corinthians 6:16)

Let us purify ourselves from everything that contaminates body and spirit, perfecting holiness out of reverence for God. (2 Corinthians 7:1)

Stand fast therefore in the liberty wherewith Christ hath made us free, and be not entangled again with the yoke of bondage ... For, brethren, ye have been called unto liberty; only use not liberty for an occasion to the flesh, but by love serve one another. (Galatians 5:1,13)

So I say, live by the Spirit, and you will not gratify the desires of a sinful nature. For the sinful nature desires what is contrary to the Spirit, and the Spirit what is contrary to the sinful nature. (Galatians 5:16-17)

And be not drunk with wine (or high on other drugs), wherein is excess; but be filled with the Spirit. (Ephesians 5:18)

Since, then, you have been raised with Christ, set your hearts on things above, where Christ is seated at the right hand of God. Set your minds on things above, not on earthly things. For you died, and your life is now hidden with Christ in God. When Christ, who is your life, appears, then you also will appear with him in glory. Put to death, therefore, whatever belongs to your earthly nature: sexual immorality, impurity, lust, evil desires and greed, which is idolatry. (Colossians 3:1-5)

For we do not have a high priest who is unable to sympathize with our weaknesses, but we have one who has been tempted in every way, just as we are--yet was without sin. Let us then approach the throne of grace with confidence, so that we may receive mercy and find grace to help us in our time of need. (Hebrews 4:15-16)

A man is a slave to whatever has mastered him. (2 Peter 2:19)

CHAPTER THREE

The "it" of Compulsiveness

DEFINITION: Compulsiveness is the irresistible impulse to do irrational, repetitive, sinful, or unnecessary actions.

FACTS ABOUT COMPULSIVENESS:

Examples of compulsiveness include compulsive gambling, addictions, sex, eating, talking, hording, drinking and working. These are examples of uncontrolled works of the flesh. An activity may be harmless in itself, but may become compulsive behavior when it is done excessively and repeatedly.

Compulsiveness is a lack of self-discipline. As a follower of Christ, self-control should be one of the spiritual attributes apparent in your life. *"But the fruit of the Spirit is love, joy, peace, patience, kindness, goodness, faithfulness, gentleness and self-control" (Galatians 5:22-23).*

An anxiety disorder called obsessive compulsive disorder (OCD) is characterized by obsessive thoughts that lead to compulsive and repetitive behavior.

The root cause of compulsiveness is anxiety. People often eat because they are stressed. They talk excessively when they are upset. They gamble and drink to find relief from their anxieties. Such behaviors reflect a lack of trust in God and His promises of care and provision. This leads to compulsive behaviors such as sex, overeating, alcoholism, etc., to attempt to deal with the complexities of life.

Compulsiveness is sin. You are commanded to refrain from worry, so therefore compulsive anxiety over the circumstances of life is sin (Matthew 6:31-34; Philippians 4:6). You are also commanded to show self-control, and when you are acting compulsively and out of control, you are not doing so

DEALING WITH COMPULSIVENESS:

Repent of compulsive behavior. Compulsiveness is a lack of self-control. Confess it to God as sin and ask forgiveness.

Ask God to give you strength to deal with compulsive behavior. Whether your problem is compulsive anxiety, gambling, sex, eating, talking, hording, drinking--God will give you strength to conquer these.

Pray about your concerns instead of worrying about them. Philippians 4:6-7 commands you to pray about everything instead of worrying.

Flee temptation. Do not put yourself in a place where you will be tempted. For example, if you are a compulsive gambler, do not go to a gambling casino. If you have problems with compulsive eating, a restaurant with a buffet is probably not the best choice for you.
Put off the works of the flesh and put on the Fruit of the Holy Spirit. See Galatians (6:19-25). Learn to live in the Spirit instead of according to the dictates of your flesh that lead to compulsive behavior.

Do not allow yourself to be brought under the power of anything other than God. Paul said that everything was permissible, but that he would not permit himself to be overpowered by anything (1 Corinthians 6:12). For example, eating is good because it maintains life, but gluttony means your eating is out of control.

Renew your mind in the Word of God. As with most issues of spiritual life, the battle begins and is fought and won in your mind. Transform your mind by studying the Word of God. (Romans 12:1-2). When obsessive thoughts try to return, rebuke them in the name of Jesus using the Word of God. Take control of your thought life. Cast down vain worries and anxieties (1 Corinthians 10:4-5)

When you find yourself engaging in compulsive behavior again, stop immediately! Ask God for forgiveness and stop doing what you are doing. Use your spiritual weapons to defeat Satan right then and there!

WHAT GOD'S WORD SAYS ABOUT COMPULSIVENESS:

So, do not worry, saying, 'What shall we eat?' or 'What shall we drink?' or 'What shall we wear?' For the pagans run after all these things, and your heavenly Father knows that you need them. But seek first his kingdom and his righteousness, and all these things will be given to you as well. Therefore, do not worry about tomorrow, for tomorrow will worry about itself. Each day has enough trouble of its own. (Matthew 6:31-34)

Therefore, I urge you, brothers, in view of God's mercy, to offer your bodies as living sacrifices, holy and pleasing to God--this is your spiritual act of worship. Do not conform any longer to the pattern of this world, but be transformed by the renewing of your mind. Then you will be able to test and approve what God's will is--his good, pleasing and perfect will. (Romans 12:1-2)

Let us behave decently, as in the daytime, not in orgies and drunkenness, not in sexual immorality and debauchery, not in dissension and jealousy. Rather, clothe yourselves with the Lord Jesus Christ, and do not think about how to gratify the desires of the sinful nature. (Romans 13:14)

Everything is permissible for me-but not everything is beneficial. Everything is permissible for me-but I will not be mastered by anything. (1 Corinthians 6:12)

For the weapons of our warfare are not carnal but mighty in God for pulling down strongholds, casting down arguments and every high thing that exalts itself against the knowledge of God, bringing every thought into captivity to the obedience of Christ, (1 Corinthians 10:4-5)

No temptation has seized you except what is common to man. And God is faithful; he will not let you be tempted beyond what you can bear. But when you are tempted, he will also provide a way out so that you can stand up under it. (1 Corinthians 10:13)

But the fruit of the Spirit is love, joy, peace, patience, kindness, goodness, faithfulness, gentleness and self-control. (Galatians 5:22-23).

Do not be anxious about anything, but in everything, by prayer and petition, with thanksgiving, present your requests to God. And the peace of God, which transcends all understanding, will guard your hearts and your minds in Christ Jesus. (Philippians 4:6-7)

Cast all your anxiety on him because he cares for you. (1 Peter 5:6)

CHAPTER FOUR

The "it" of Habits

DEFINITION: A habit is a routine behavior that is repeated regularly and tends to occur unconsciously. It is a fixed way of thinking, feeling, and acting.

FACTS ABOUT HABITS:

There are good and bad habits. All habits are not bad. Habits like a daily devotional time, prayer, and study of God's Word are good habits to foster. Bad habits are the problems for which you should seek change.

Some examples of bad habits are addictions, laziness, being critical, gossiping, selfishness, cursing, etc. For believers, bad habits are anything that turn you from God and lead you to respond in an unbiblical way.

Habits begin in the mind. Lust conceives the thought, the thought becomes an action, and the repeated action becomes a sinful habit (James 1:13-15). Guard your thoughts because they become words and actions, these become habits, and habits affect your character.

Bad habits become strongholds. Spiritually speaking, a stronghold is anything that exalts itself against the knowledge of God (2 Corinthians 10:3-5). A stronghold is a spiritual point of operation from where Satan can attack you further. Strongholds include things like sinful attitudes and addictions as well as habits that enslave you and result in you doing what you don't want to do.

Habits can be changed. The Bible says: *"Therefore, if anyone is in Christ, he is a new creation; the old has gone, the new has come!" (2 Corinthians 5:17-18).* Your spiritual weapons, described in Ephesians 6, have supernatural power to demolish strongholds (2 Corinthians 10:3-5).

DEALING WITH HABITS:

Take personal responsibility for your bad habits. Do not blame someone else because they modeled or taught you such behavior.

Analyze the root cause of your bad habit. Why are you doing what you are doing? When did you develop this habit?   For example, did you start smoking because everyone else was doing it? Discovering why you are doing something will help you conquer it.

Pray about your habits. Confess sinful habits it to God, ask forgiveness, and claim His strength to help you overcome it (Philippians 4:13).

Put off old habits and replace them with new. For each bad habit, attitude, or behavior that the Bible admonishes you to put off, you are also admonished to "put on" good ones to replace them. This means you deliberately--by a decision of your mind--cultivate the opposite of your negative behaviors. See Appendix Three of this database for behaviors the Bible mandates believers to put off and the new qualities that are to replace them. Focus on building good habits rather than eliminating the bad (Ephesians 4:22-24).

Renew your mind in the Word of God. Habitual behavior begins in the mind. It starts as a decision to act or think in a certain way. As you renew your mind with the Word of God, you will be transformed and break the power of bad habits (Romans 12:1-2).

Use the buddy system. If you are trying to break a bad habit like smoking or binge eating, find someone else who is wanting to eliminate the same habit and encourage one another in the process (James 5:16).

Conquer your bad habits in the strength of the Lord. Philippians 4:13 declares that you can do all things through the strength given by Jesus Christ. Hebrews 4:15-16 states that you will have help in times of need.

Develop positive spiritual habits. Habits like a daily devotional time, prayer, and study of God's Word are excellent habits to foster.

Use your spiritual weapons when Satan tempts you to resume old habits (Ephesians 6 and 2 Corinthians 10:4-5). These weapons have supernatural power to demolish strongholds. Submit yourself to God, resist the devil, and he will flee (James 4:7).

WHAT GOD'S WORD SAYS ABOUT HABITS:

Therefore, I urge you, brothers, in view of God's mercy, to offer your bodies as living sacrifices, holy and pleasing to God--this is your spiritual act of worship. Do not conform any longer to the pattern of this world, but be transformed by the renewing of your mind. Then you will be able to test and approve what God's will is--his good, pleasing and perfect will. (Romans 12:1-2)

Don't you know that you yourselves are God's temple and that God's Spirit lives in you? If anyone destroys God's temple, God will destroy him; for God's temple is sacred, and you are that temple. (1 Corinthians 3:16-17)

Do you not know that your body is a temple of the Holy Spirit, who is in you, whom you have received from God? You are not your own; you were bought at a price. Therefore, honor God with your body. (1 Corinthians 6:19-20)

Therefore, if anyone is in Christ, he is a new creation; the old has gone, the new has come! (2 Corinthians 5:17-18)

The weapons we fight with are not the weapons of the world. On the contrary, they have divine power to demolish strongholds. We demolish arguments and every pretension that sets itself up against the knowledge of God, and we take captive every thought to make it obedient to Christ (2 Corinthians 10:3-5)

But he said to me, "My grace is sufficient for you, for my power is made perfect in weakness." Therefore, I will boast all the more gladly about my weaknesses, so that Christ's power may rest on me. That is why, for Christ's sake, I delight in weaknesses, in insults, in hardships, in persecutions, in difficulties. For when I am weak, then I am strong. (2 Corinthians 12:9-10)

You were taught, with regard to your former way of life, to put off your old self, which is being corrupted by its deceitful desires; to be made new in the attitude of your minds; and to put on the new self, created to be like God in true righteousness and holiness. (Ephesians 4:22-24)

I can do everything through him who gives me strength. (Philippians 4:13)

For we do not have a high priest who is unable to sympathize with our weaknesses, but we have one who has been tempted in every way, just as we are--yet was without sin. Let us then approach the throne of grace with confidence, so that we may receive mercy and find grace to help us in our time of need. (Hebrews 4:15-16)

When tempted, no one should say, "God is tempting me." For God cannot be tempted by evil, nor does he tempt anyone; but each one is tempted when, by his own evil desire, he is dragged away and enticed. Then, after desire has conceived, it gives birth to sin; and sin, when it is full-grown, gives birth to death. (James 1:13-15)

Submit yourselves, then, to God. Resist the devil, and he will flee from you. (James 4:7)

If we claim to be without sin, we deceive ourselves and the truth is not in us. If we confess our sins, he is faithful and just and will forgive us our sins and purify us from all unrighteousness. If we claim we have not sinned, we make him out to be a liar and his word has no place in our lives. (1 John 1:8-10)

CHAPTER FIVE

The "it" of the Mind and Thoughts

DEFINITION: The part of a person that thinks, reasons, feels, and remembers.

FACTS ABOUT THE MIND AND THOUGHTS:

The mind is complex. The mind is one of the most complex and least understood parts of the human body.

Satan uses many strategies against your mind. These include questioning the authority of God, deception, seduction, lust, depression, discouragement, rebellion, and wrong attitudes, emotions, and motives. Satan also accuses and condemns, causes confusion, and promotes compromise, rebellion, and tormenting thoughts like fear. Satan also blinds the minds of unbelievers.

What you program into your mind affects your thinking. What you watch, listen to, read, and the people with whom you interact--these all affect your thinking.

God wants you to have a victorious mind. He wants you to have the mind of Christ (1 Corinthians 2:16).

DEALING WITH THE MIND AND THOUGHTS:

Ask forgiveness for wrong thinking. If you have been thinking negative and/or sinful thoughts, ask God to forgive you.

Guard what you see and hear. Do not program negative and sinful things into your mind. Do not let your mind become a dumping ground for dirty jokes and gossip.

Take control of your thoughts.   The Bible says that as believers *"We demolish arguments and every pretension that sets itself up against the knowledge of God, and we take captive every thought to make it obedient to Christ" (2 Corinthians 10:5).*

Set your mind on God by immersing yourself in His Word. Isaiah 26:3 declares: *"You will keep in perfect peace him whose mind is steadfast, because he trusts in you."*

WHAT GOD'S WORD SAYS ABOUT THE MIND THOUGHTS:

May the words of my mouth and the meditation of my heart be pleasing in your sight, O Lord, my Rock and my Redeemer. (Psalm 19:14)

Test me, O Lord, and try me, examine my heart and my mind; for your love is ever before me, and I walk continually in your truth. (Psalm 26:2-3)

You will keep in perfect peace him whose mind is steadfast, because he trusts in you. (Isaiah 26:3)

Yet you know me, O Lord; you see me and test my thoughts about you. (Jeremiah 12:3)

The good man brings good things out of the good stored up in his heart, and the evil man brings evil things out of the evil stored up in his heart. For out of the overflow of his heart his mouth speaks. (Luke 6:45)

Those who live in accordance with the Spirit have their minds set on what the Spirit desires. (Romans 8:5)

But we have the mind of Christ. (1 Corinthians 2:16)

We demolish arguments and every pretension that sets itself up against the knowledge of God, and we take captive every thought to make it obedient to Christ. (2 Corinthians 10:5)

When I was a child, I talked like a child; I thought like a child, I reasoned like a child. When I became a man, I put childish ways behind me. (1 Corinthians 13:11)

Brothers, stop thinking like children. In regard to evil be infants, but in your thinking, be adults. (I Corinthians 14:20)

We demolish arguments and every pretension that sets itself up against the knowledge of God, and we take captive every thought to make it obedient to Christ. (2 Corinthians 10:5)

Forgetting what is behind and straining toward what is ahead, I press on toward the goal to win the prize for which God has called me heavenward in Christ Jesus. (Philippians 3:13-14)

Finally, brothers, whatever is true, whatever is noble, whatever is right, whatever is lovely, whatever is admirable--if anything is excellent or praiseworthy, think about such things. (Philippians 4:8)

Watch your life and doctrine closely. (1 Timothy 4:16)

All Scripture is God-breathed and is useful for teaching, rebuking, correcting and training in righteousness, so that the man of God may be thoroughly equipped for every good work. (2 Timothy 3:16-17)

Therefore, holy brothers, who share in the heavenly calling, fix your thoughts on Jesus. (Hebrews 3:1)

For the word of God is living and active. Sharper than any double-edged sword, it penetrates even to dividing soul and spirit, joints and marrow; it judges the thoughts and attitudes of the heart. (Hebrews 4:12)

Improper Thinking.

In his pride the wicked does not seek him; in all his thoughts there is no room for God. (Psalm 10:4)

How long must I wrestle with my thoughts and every day have sorrow in my heart? ... But I trust in your unfailing love; my heart rejoices in your salvation. (Psalm 13:2-6)

The Lord detests the thoughts of the wicked, but those of the pure are pleasing to him. (Proverbs 15:26)

Let the wicked forsake his way and the evil man his thoughts. (Isaiah 55:7)

Wash the evil from your heart and be saved. How long will you harbor wicked thoughts? (Jeremiah 4:14)

For out of the heart come evil thoughts, murder, adultery, sexual immorality, theft, false testimony, slander. These are what make a man "unclean"; but eating with unwashed hands does not make him "unclean."(Matthew 15:19-20)

Jesus replied: "'Love the Lord your God with all your heart and with all your soul and with all your mind.' This is the first and greatest commandment." (Matthew 22:37-38)

For although they knew God, they neither glorified him as God nor gave thanks to him, but their thinking became futile and their foolish hearts were darkened. (Romans 1:21)

Those who live according to the sinful nature have their minds set on what that nature desires. The sinful mind is hostile to God. It does not submit to God's law, nor can it do so. The mind of sinful man is death, but the mind controlled by the Spirit is life and peace. (Romans 8:5-7)

Do not conform any longer to the pattern of this world, but be transformed by the renewing of your mind. Then you will be able to test and approve what God's will is his good, pleasing and perfect will. (Romans 12:2)

Many live as enemies of the cross of Christ. Their destiny is destruction, their god is their stomach, and their glory is their shame. Their mind is on earthly things. (Philippians 3:18-19)

Negative mindsets to avoid.
-A carnal mind: Romans 8:6-7
-A mind alienated from God: Colossians 1:21
-A defiled mind: Titus 1:15
-A fleshly mind: Ephesians 2:3
-A hardened mind: Daniel 5:20
-A doubtful mind: Luke 12:29
-A vain mind: Ephesians 4:17
-A blinded mind: 2 Corinthians 3:14

-A seared mind and conscience: Titus 1:15
-A despiteful mind: Ezekiel 36:5
-An evil mind: Acts 14:2
-An unbelieving mind: 2 Corinthians 4:4
-A fainting mind: Hebrews 12:3
-A reprobate mind: 2 Timothy 3:8
-A double minded mind: James 1:8; 4:8
-A corrupt mind: 1 Timothy 6:5; 2 Timothy 3:8; 2 Corinthians 11:3
-A reprobate mind: Romans 1:28-32.

Positive mental qualities to develop:
-A ready mind: 2 Corinthians 8:19; 1 Peter 5:2; Acts 17:11
-A pure mind: 2 Peter 3:1
-A stayed mind: Isaiah 26:3
-A renewed mind: Ephesians 4:23; Romans 12:2
-A humble mind: Colossians 3:12; Acts 20:19
-A sober mind: Titus 2:6
-A sound mind: 2 Timothy 1:7
-A mind of love: Matthew 22:37
-A serving mind: Romans 7:25
-A fully persuaded mind: Romans 14:5
-A fervent mind: 2 Corinthians 7:7
-A willing mind: 2 Corinthians 8:12

CHAPTER SIX

The "it" of Trials, Troubles, Adversities

DEFINITION: A trial is an examination by testing. Biblically, it is a test of faith in which you experience trouble or adversity. Trouble is sometimes referred to as "tribulation" in the Bible. Adversity is similar to trouble, meaning extremely unfavorable experiences.

FACTS ABOUT TRIALS, TROUBLES, AND ADVERSITIES:

A trial is not a temptation. A temptation is something that entices you to sin (see the topic of "Temptation" in this database). A trial is an adversity you are experiencing that tests your faith.

Trials, troubles, and adversities are experienced by all believers. In fact, the apostles taught believers that they would only enter the Kingdom of God through adversity (Acts 14:22). Peter said not to consider it strange or unusual when you encounter trouble (1 Peter 4:12).

God uses both positive and negative experiences for your good. Joseph told his brothers: *"You intended to harm me, but God intended it for good to accomplish what is now being done, the saving of many lives" (Genesis 50:20).* The Apostle Paul declared: *"And we know that in all things God works for the good of those who love him, who have been called according to his purpose" (Romans 8:28)*

DEALING WITH TRIALS, TROUBLES, AND ADVERSITIES:

Expect to experience adversity. Peter said not to be surprised by it (1 Peter 4:12-16). The apostles taught the early church that it was to be experienced as part of living in the Kingdom of God (Acts 14:22).

Pray about your trials, troubles and adversities. The Bible says that God has promised to hear before you call and even while you are yet speaking (Isaiah 65:24). Confess your total dependence on Him. Instead of asking "What am I going to do in this adversity?" ask God, "What are You going to do?"

Immerse yourself in the Word of God. The Bible brings comfort and direction during trials, troubles, and adversities.

Use your spiritual weapons. Trials, troubles, and adverse circumstances must be faced with your spiritual weapons. Study Ephesians 6:10-18. See also "Spiritual Warfare" in this database.

Remember that good things come from God. If something comes to rob, steal, or destroy in your life, do not blame God. It is from the enemy. Jesus said: *"The thief comes only to steal and kill and destroy; I have come that they may have life, and have it to the full" (John 10:10).* James said: *"Don't be deceived, my dear brothers. Every good and perfect gift is from above, coming down from the Father of the heavenly lights, who does not change like shifting shadows" (James 1:16-17).*

35

Remember that there is divine purpose in adversity. Your faith is being refined (1 Peter 1:6-7) and spiritual qualities are being developed in your life: *"Not only so, but we also rejoice in our sufferings, because we know that suffering produces perseverance; perseverance, character; and character, hope" (Romans 5:3-4).*

Focus on eternal benefits. The Bible indicates that trials actually work for you when you are focused on the eternal benefits of the trials instead of the temporary problems: *"Therefore we do not lose heart. Even though our outward man is perishing, yet the inward man is being renewed day by day. For our light affliction, which is but for a moment, is working for us a far more exceeding and eternal weight of glory, while we do not look at the things which are seen, but at the things which are not seen. For the things which are seen are temporary, but the things which are not seen are eternal" (2 Corinthians 4:16-18).*

Rejoice in times of adversity. The Bible commands you to rejoice and give thanks to God in times of adversity.   You may not feel like doing this, but do it as an act of your will (See 1 Thessalonians 5:18 and 1 Peter 1:6-7; 4:12-17). You do not give thanks for the adversity, but in the midst of and in spite of it.

Remember these six "p"s of adversity.
   -Purpose: God has divine purpose in your trial.
   -Profitable: Your trial is profitable if you submit to God and trust Him.
   -Presence: God will be with you in your trials.
   -Prove: Your faith will be proven by the difficulties.
   -Produce: Your trial will produce positive spiritual qualities in your life.
   -Perspective: You will emerge with a new perspective.

WHAT GOD'S WORD SAYS ABOUT TRIALS, TROUBLES, AND ADVERSITIES:

You intended to harm me, but God intended it for good to accomplish what is now being done, the saving of many lives. (Genesis 50:20)

But in their distress, they turned to the Lord, the God of Israel, and sought him, and he was found by them. (2 Chronicles 15:4)

Have I not commanded you? Be strong and courageous. Do not be terrified; do not be discouraged, for the Lord your God will be with you wherever you go. (Joshua 1:9)

The Lord is a refuge for the oppressed, a stronghold in times of trouble. (Psalm 9:9)

Do not be far from me, for trouble is near and there is no one to help. (Psalm 22:11)

The troubles of my heart have multiplied; free me from my anguish. (Psalm 25:17)

For in the day of trouble he will keep me safe in his dwelling; he will hide me in the shelter of his tabernacle and set me high upon a rock. (Psalm 27:5)

I will be glad and rejoice in your love, for you saw my affliction and knew the anguish of my soul. You have not handed me over to the enemy but have set my feet in a spacious place. (Psalm 31:8)

You are my hiding place; you will protect me from trouble and surround me with songs of deliverance. (Psalm 32:7)

This poor man called, and the Lord heard him; he saved him out of all his troubles. The angel of the Lord encamps around those who fear him, and he delivers them. (Psalm 34:6)

The righteous cry out, and the Lord hears them; he delivers them from all their troubles. The Lord is close to the brokenhearted and saves those who are crushed in spirit. A righteous man may have many troubles, but the Lord delivers him from them all. (Psalm 34:17-19)

May all who gloat over my distress be put to shame and confusion. (Psalm 35:26)

The salvation of the righteous comes from the Lord; he is their stronghold in time of trouble. The Lord helps them and delivers them; he delivers them from the wicked and saves them, because they take refuge in him. (Psalm 37:39-40)

For troubles without number surround me; my sins have overtaken me, and I cannot see. They are more than the hairs of my head, and my heart fails within me. (Psalm 40:12)

God is our refuge and strength, an ever-present help in trouble. (Psalm 46:1)

...call upon me in the day of trouble; I will deliver you, and you will honor me. (Psalm 50:15)

But I will sing of your strength, in the morning I will sing of your love; for you are my fortress, my refuge in times of trouble. (Psalms 59:16)

Do not hide your face from your servant; answer me quickly, for I am in trouble. (Psalm 69:17)

In the day of my trouble I will call to you, for you will answer me. (Psalm 86:7)

He will call upon me, and I will answer him; I will be with him in trouble, I will deliver him and honor him. (Psalms 91:15)

Do not hide your face from me when I am in distress. Turn your ear to me; when I call, answer me quickly. (Psalms 102:2)

Give us aid against the enemy, for the help of man is worthless. With God we will gain the victory, and he will trample down our enemies. (Psalms 108:12-13)

Trouble and distress have come upon me, but your commands are my delight. (Psalm 119:143)

Though I walk in the midst of trouble, you preserve my life; you stretch out your hand against the anger of my foes, with your right hand you save me. The Lord will fulfill [his purpose] for me; your love, O Lord, endures forever--do not abandon the works of your hands. (Psalms 138:7-8)

I pour out my complaint before him; before him I tell my trouble. (Psalm 142:2)

For your name's sake, O Lord, preserve my life; in your righteousness, bring me out of trouble. (Psalms 143:11)

If you falter in times of trouble, how small is your strength! (Proverbs 24:10)

For I am the Lord, your God, who takes hold of your right hand and says to you, do not fear; I will help you. (Isaiah 41:13)

Shout for joy, O heavens; rejoice O earth; burst into song, O mountains! For the Lord comforts his people and will have compassion on his afflicted ones. (Isaiah 49:13)

... no weapon forged against you will prevail, and you will refute every tongue that accuses you. (Isaiah 54:17)

Before they call I will answer; while they are still speaking I will hear. (Isaiah 65:24)

The Lord is good, A stronghold in the day of trouble; And He knows those who trust in Him. (Nahum 1:7)

The thief comes only to steal and kill and destroy; I have come that they may have life, and have it to the full. (John 10:10)

Do not let your hearts be troubled and do not be afraid. (John 14:27)

In this world you will have trouble. But take heart! I have overcome the world. (John 16:33)

They preached the good news in that city and won many disciples. Then they returned to Lystra, Iconium and Antioch, strengthening the disciples and encouraging them to remain true to the faith. "We must go through many hardships to enter the kingdom of God," they said. (Acts 14:22)

Not only so, but we also rejoice in our sufferings, because we know that suffering produces perseverance; perseverance, character; and character, hope. (Romans 5:3-4).

And we know that in all things God works for the good of those who love him, who have been called according to his purpose. (Romans 8:28)

Who shall separate us from the love of Christ? Shall trouble or hardship or persecution or famine or nakedness or danger or sword? As it is written: "For your sake we face death all day long;

we are considered as sheep to be slaughtered."   No, in all these things we are more than conquerors through him who loved us. For I am convinced that neither death nor life, neither angels nor demons, neither the present nor the future, nor any powers, neither height nor depth, nor anything else in all creation, will be able to separate us from the love of God that is in Christ Jesus our Lord. (Romans 8:35-39)

Be joyful in hope, patient in affliction, and faithful in prayer. (Romans 12:12)

Praise be to the God and Father of our Lord Jesus Christ, the Father of compassion and the God of all comfort, who comforts us in all our troubles, so that we can comfort those in any trouble with the comfort we ourselves have received from God. For just as the sufferings of Christ flow over into our lives, so also through Christ our comfort overflows. (2 Corinthians 1:3-5)

Therefore, we do not lose heart. Even though our outward man is perishing, yet the inward man is being renewed day by day. For our light affliction, which is but for a moment, is working for us a far more exceeding and eternal weight of glory, while we do not look at the things which are seen, but at the things which are not seen. For the things which are seen are temporary, but the things which are not seen are eternal. (2 Corinthians 4:16-18)

But he said to me, "My grace is sufficient for you, for my power is made perfect in weakness." Therefore, I will boast all the more gladly about my weaknesses, so that Christ's power may rest on me. That is why, for Christ's sake, I delight in weaknesses, in insults, in hardships, in persecutions, in difficulties. For when I am weak, then I am strong. (2 Corinthians 12:9)

Do not be anxious about anything, but in everything, by prayer and petition, with thanksgiving, present your requests to God. And the peace of God, which transcends all understanding, will guard your hearts and your minds in Christ Jesus. (Philippians 4:6-7)

... that no one should be shaken by these afflictions; for you yourselves know that we are appointed to this. (1 Thessalonians 3:3, NKJV)

Give thanks in all circumstances, for this is God's will for you in Christ Jesus. (1 Thessalonians 5:18)

Blessed is the man who perseveres under trial, because when he has stood the test, he will receive the crown of life that God has promised to those who love him. (James 1:12)

Don't be deceived, my dear brothers. Every good and perfect gift is from above, coming down from the Father of the heavenly lights, who does not change like shifting shadows. (James 1:16-17).

Is any one of you in trouble? He should pray. (James 5:13)

In this you greatly rejoice, though now for a little while you may have had to suffer grief in all kinds of trials. These have come so that your faith--of greater worth than gold, which perishes even though refined by fire--may be proved genuine and may result in praise, glory and honor when Jesus Christ is revealed. (1 Peter 1:6-7)

Dear friends, do not be surprised at the painful trial you are suffering, as though something strange were happening to you. But rejoice that you participate in the sufferings of Christ, so that you may be overjoyed when his glory is revealed. If you are insulted because of the name of Christ, you are blessed, for the Spirit of glory and of God rests on you. If you suffer, it should not be as a murderer or thief or any other kind of criminal, or even as a meddler. However, if you suffer as a Christian, do not be ashamed, but praise God that you bear that name. (1 Peter 4:12-17)

Cast all your anxiety on him because he cares for you. Be self-controlled and alert. Your enemy the devil prowls around like a roaring lion looking for someone to devour. Resist him, standing firm in the faith, because you know that your brothers throughout the world are undergoing the same kind of sufferings. And the God of all grace, who called you to his eternal glory in Christ, after you have suffered a little while, will himself restore you and make you strong, firm and steadfast. (1 Peter 5:7-10)

Study the story of Job--especially chapters 1-2 and chapter 42--to understand more about the purpose of trials.

CHAPTER SEVEN

The "it" of Peer Pressure

DEFINITION: Peer pressure is the influence that a group or an individual exerts over someone that encourages them to change their attitudes, values, or behaviors to conform to group norms.

FACTS ABOUT PEER PRESSURE:

There are both positive and negative influences in life. You must make decisions each day about which of these you will allow to influence you. Positive peer pressure that encourages you to do good is not a problem. It is the negative peer pressure of ungodly influences in your life which you must learn to confront and conquer.

You are influenced by those with whom you associate. The Bible *says, "Do not be misled: Bad company corrupts good character" (1 Corinthians 15:33).* Proverbs warns: *"Do not make friends with a hot-tempered man, do not associate with one easily angered, or you may learn his ways and get yourself ensnared" (Proverbs 22:24-25).* Substitute any negative influence for the words "hot-tempered" and the result is the same--if you run with someone who is dishonest, you learn their ways. If you hang out with a liar, you will become one too.

You should be an example instead of following bad examples. Paul told a young believer named Timothy: *"Don't let anyone look down on you because you are young, but set an example for the believers in speech, in life, in love, in faith and in purity" (1 Timothy 4:12-13).* Jesus said you were to follow His example (John 13:15) and that as a believer you are His ambassador to the world (1 Corinthians 5:20). Do not be a clone. Be an example. You are to be the salt of the earth (Matthew 5:13). Tasteless salt is worthless (Mark 9:50). As a follower of Christ, it is your responsibility to flavor the world around you, so it will be positively impacted for God.

Doing things because "everyone else is doing them" is idolatry. The Lord said that Israel imitated the sinful nations around them, although God had ordered them not to do so. They followed idolatrous people and became idolatrous themselves (2 Kings 17:15). When you decide to do something because "everyone else is doing it", you are establishing those unsaved people as an idol in your life--imitating them and adhering to their standards instead of following God.

DEALING WITH PEER PRESSURE:

Do not blame God when you yield to peer pressure. The Bible says: *"When tempted, no one should say, 'God is tempting me.' For God cannot be tempted by evil, nor does he tempt anyone; but each one is tempted when, by his own evil desire, he is dragged away and enticed. Then, after desire has conceived, it gives birth to sin; and sin, when it is full-grown, gives birth to death" (James 1:13-15).*

Repent of conforming to negative peer pressure. If you have been yielding to pressure to do things that are not in harmony with God's Word, you have sinned. Confess, repent, and ask God to forgive you.

Rebuke the fear of man. The Bible says that the fear of man is a spiritual snare which entraps you in their ways (Proverbs 29:25).

Determine that you will obey God rather than man. The disciples took their stand against "peer pressure", even when facing possible imprisonment and death.   Peter and the other apostles declared: *"We must obey God rather than men!" (Acts 5:29).*

Renew your mind in the Word of God. This will enable you to be transformed instead of conforming to the world (Romans 12:1-2).

Do not be unequally yoked in relationships. The Bible warns believers*: "Do not be yoked together with unbelievers. For what do righteousness and wickedness have in common? Or what fellowship can light have with darkness? What harmony is there between Christ and Belial? What does a believer have in common with an unbeliever? What agreement is there between the temple of God and idols? For we are the temple of the living God. As God has said: "I will live with them and walk among them, and I will be their God, and they will be my people." "Therefore, come out from them and be separate," says the Lord. "Touch no unclean thing, and I will receive you. I will be a Father to you, and you will be my sons and daughters" (2 Corinthians 6:14-18).*   Break close relationships with those who exert pressure for you to look, act, think, or talk in ways that are not in harmony with God's Word.

Form positive relationships. Make friends with fellow-believers who are seeking to live by the Word of God. You can be friendly to everyone, but your close relationships should be with those who have like spiritual goals. Find friends at church, at Bible study groups, or through Christian social organizations. Find a prayer partner as well, one with whom you can pray regularly.

Do not become involved in the troubles of others. Some people want to involve you in their messes and even take delight in getting you into trouble. The moment you are tempted to become involved in another person's issues, you end up as part of their troubles. The Bible warns: *"Enter not into the path of the wicked, and go not in the way of evil men. Avoid it, pass not by it, turn from it, and pass away. For they sleep not, except they have done mischief; and their sleep is taken away, unless they cause some to fall. For they eat the bread of wickedness, and drink the wine of violence" (Proverbs 4:14-17, KJV).*

WHAT GOD'S WORD SAYS ABOUT PEER PRESSURE:

Do not follow the crowd in doing wrong. (Exodus 23:2)

Blessed is the man who does not walk in the counsel of the wicked or stand in the way of sinners or sit in the seat of mockers. But his delight is in the law of the Lord, and on his law he meditates day and night. (Psalm 1:1-2)

Away from me, you evildoers, that I may keep the commands of my God! (Psalm 119:115)

My son, if sinners entice you, does not give in to them. If they say, "Come along with us;
let's lie in wait for someone's blood, let's waylay some harmless soul; let's swallow them alive,
like the grave, and whole, like those who go down to the pit; we will get all sorts of valuable
things and fill our houses with plunder; throw in your lot with us, and we will share a common
purse"--my son, do not go along with them, do not set foot on their paths; for their feet rush into
sin, they are swift to shed blood. (Proverbs 1:10-16)

Enter not into the path of the wicked, and go not in the way of evil men. Avoid it, pass not by it,
turn from it, and pass away. For they sleep not, except they have done mischief; and their sleep is
taken away, unless they cause some to fall. For they eat the bread of wickedness, and drink the
wine of violence. (Proverbs 4:14-17. KJV)

Do not make friends with a hot-tempered man, do not associate with one easily angered, or you
may learn his ways and get yourself ensnared. (Proverbs 22:24-25)

Do not join those who drink too much wine or gorge themselves on meat, for drunkards and
gluttons become poor, and drowsiness clothes them in rags. (Proverbs 23:20-21)

Fear of man will prove to be a snare, but whoever trusts in the Lord is kept safe. (Proverbs
29:25)

Peter and the other apostles replied: "We must obey God rather than men!" (Acts 5:29)

Therefore, I urge you, brothers, in view of God's mercy, to offer your bodies as living sacrifices,
holy and pleasing to God--this is your spiritual act of worship. Do not conform any longer to the
pattern of this world, but be transform. (Romans 12:1-2)

Do not be yoked together with unbelievers. For what do righteousness and wickedness have in
common? Or what fellowship can light have with darkness? What harmony is there between
Christ and Belial? What does a believer have in common with an unbeliever? What agreement is
there between the temple of God and idols? For we are the temple of the living God. As God has
said: "I will live with them and walk among them, and I will be their God, and they will be my
people." "Therefore, come out from them and be separate," says the Lord. "Touch no unclean
thing, and I will receive you. I will be a Father to you, and you will be my sons and daughters.
(2 Corinthians 6:14-18)

Do not be misled: Bad company corrupts good character. (1 Corinthians 15:33)

Am I now trying to win the approval of men, or of God? Or am I trying to please men? If I were
still trying to please men, I would not be a servant of Christ. (Galatians 1:10)

Don't let anyone look down on you because you are young, but set an example for the believers
in speech, in life, in love, in faith and in purity. (1Timothy 4:12-13)
When tempted, no one should say, "God is tempting me." For God cannot be tempted by evil,
nor does he tempt anyone; but each one is tempted when, by his own evil desire, he is dragged

away and enticed. Then, after desire has conceived, it gives birth to sin; and sin, when it is full-grown, gives birth to death. (James 1:13-15)

CHAPTER EIGHT

The "it" of Chastening and Discipline

DEFINITION: Chastening means to discipline in order to correct errors or faults.

FACTS ABOUT CHASTENING AND DISCIPLINE:

Reasons for chastening and discipline. It is the nature of sin to rebel against authority. This is what caused the original sin of Lucifer (Satan) and of man (Adam and Eve). Because of this basic sin nature, we all rebel and need correction at times.

Pastors or spiritual leaders have the authority for discipline within a church or ministry because they have the responsibility for the spiritual welfare of followers (Hebrews 13:7). You are to respond positively to your spiritual leaders, so it will be a joy for them to lead you.

God expects parents to discipline their children. The Bible says that a person without discipline will die without instruction--spiritual death for sure, and maybe even physical death (Proverbs 5:23). Proverbs 23:13 says *"do not withhold discipline from a child."* Moses commanded Israel to teach their children to observe all of God's words (Deuteronomy 32:46). The Bible says: *"Fathers, do not provoke your children to anger, but bring them up in the discipline and instruction of the Lord" (Ephesians 6:4, NASU).*

God disciplines believers through His Word, trials of faith, and adverse circumstances.

The purposes of chastening and discipline. It leads you to repentance and corrects sin (1 Corinthians 8:9; 2 Corinthians 7:9). It keeps you humble (2 Corinthians 12:7-9). It teaches you spiritual discernment (1 Corinthians 11:31-32) and to obey God's Word (Psalm 119:67). It encourages you to be faithful (1 Corinthians 5:6-7); protects the testimony of the church (1 Timothy 3:7); and is restorative (Galatians 6:1; Matthew 6:14-15).

Chastening and discipline confirm God's love for you. It confirms that you are a child of God and that He cares about you (Hebrews 12:8, Psalms 94:12; Proverbs 3:11-12).

DEALING WITH CHASTENING AND DISCIPLINE:

Consider chastening a reason to examine your life. As the Apostle Paul admonished, *"...let a man examine himself..." (1 Corinthians 11:28).* Examine your life for sins of commission (things you should not do) and sins of omission (things you should have done but didn't).

Confess any known sin. Chastening sometimes occurs because of sin, so confess any known sin. When you do, God will cleanse you from all unrighteousness, meaning even sins of which you are not aware (1 John 1:8-9). Pray the prayer of David: *"Cleanse me from secret faults" (Psalm 19:12).*

Do not be discouraged by discipline. Know that through chastening, God confirms His love for you (Hebrews 12:7-11). You are blessed when you are disciplined by God (Psalm 94:12)

Remember what has been called the "golden rule" if you deal with situations that require discipline: *"Whatever you wish that men would do to you, do so to them" (Matthew 7:12, RSV)*. Always ask yourself:
       -What does God's Word say about this?
       -How would Jesus handle this?
       -How would I want to be treated in this situation if our positions were reversed and I was him and he was me?"

Use these biblical guidelines for discipline:

-Go first to the erring brother and solve the matter individually and personally if possible. If the erring believer will not listen to you and repent, go again with witnesses. If he still refuses to hear you, take the matter before the entire Church (Matthew 18:15-17).

-Discipline should be with a proper spirit.   Spiritually mature believers are to first judge themselves and then deal with offenders in a spirit of meekness, love, and helpfulness (Matthew 7:1-5; Romans 15:1-2; 2 Corinthians 2:6-8, and Galatians 6:1-4).

-Correction should be done with the purpose of restoring the offender who has been taken captive by Satan (2 Timothy 2:24-26).

-Opportunity should be given for the erring brother to respond. If he repents, the leader can restore him to fellowship and ministry. If the offense is serious, the offender may need to be removed from active ministry until he sets his own life and home in order. If he is rebellious and does not repent, he must be removed from leadership and possibly, the church fellowship.

-Private problems and public sins should be handled differently (Matthew 18:15-17; 1 Corinthians 5; Galatians 2:1-14; 1 Timothy 5:20). In the passage from Matthew it seems the problem was between two individuals. It was to be dealt with by enlisting the aid of other believers and, if the offender would not listen, by excluding him from fellowship. In the other passages, the problems were matters of public record, so they were dealt with publicly.

-Exercise discipline only on the basis of factual knowledge. "Hearsay" evidence is not sufficient, and there must also be two or three witnesses to an offense (Matthew 18:15-18; 1 Corinthians 5:1 and 1 Timothy 5:1,9).

-If correction is totally refused, discipline may include exclusion from the fellowship. One of the greatest gifts God has given believers is fellowship with other believers. One of the most severe punishments is withholding such fellowship (Matthew 18:15-17; 1 Corinthians 5; 2 Thessalonians 3:14; 2 John 7-11; and 3 John 9-11).

WHAT GOD'S WORD SAYS ABOUT CHASTENING AND DISCIPLINE:

Blessed is the man you discipline, Oh Lord, the man you teach from your law. (Psalms 94:12)

Before I was afflicted I went astray, but now I obey your word. (Psalm 119:67)

My son, do not despise the Lord's discipline and do not resent his rebuke, because the Lord disciplines those he loves, as a father the son he delights in. (Proverbs 3:11-12)

But if we judged ourselves, we would not come under judgment. When we are judged by the Lord, we are being disciplined so that we will not be condemned with the world.
(1 Corinthians 11:31-32)

To keep me from becoming conceited because of these surpassingly great revelations, there was given me a thorn in my flesh, a messenger of Satan, to torment me. Three times I pleaded with the Lord to take it away from me. But he said to me, "My grace is sufficient for you, for my power is made perfect in weakness." Therefore, I will boast all the more gladly about my weaknesses, so that Christ's power may rest on me. That is why, for Christ's sake, I delight in weaknesses, in insults, in hardships, in persecutions, in difficulties. For when I am weak, then I am strong. (2 Corinthians 12:7-10)

Endure hardship as discipline; God is treating you as sons. For what son is not disciplined by his father? If you are not disciplined (and everyone undergoes discipline), then you are illegitimate children and not true sons. Moreover, we have all had human fathers who disciplined us and we respected them for it. How much more should we submit to the Father of our spirits and live! Our fathers disciplined us for a little while as they thought best; but God disciplines us for our good, that we may share in his holiness. No discipline seems pleasant at the time, but painful. Later on, however, it produces a harvest of righteousness and peace for those who have been trained by it. (Hebrews 12:7-11)

CHAPTER NINE

The "it" of Temptation

DEFINITION: Biblically, temptation is a physical and/or mental desire to sin--a deep craving for something that is contrary to the Word of God.

FACTS ABOUT TEMPTATION:

God does not tempt you. You are tempted when you are drawn away by your own carnal desires. *"When tempted, no one should say, 'God is tempting me.' For God cannot be tempted by evil, nor does he tempt anyone; but each one is tempted when, by his own evil desire, he is dragged away and enticed. Then, after desire has conceived, it gives birth to sin; and sin, when it is full-grown, gives birth to death" (James 1:13-15).* The process of temptation is desire, conception, birth, sin, and death.

The battle with temptation begins in your mind. It starts with desire which conceives evil and gives birth to sin.

Temptation arises from three major sources. The lust of the flesh, the lust of the eyes, the pride of life: *"Do not love the world or the things in the world. If anyone loves the world, the love of the Father is not in him. For all that is in the world--the lust of the flesh, the lust of the eyes, and the pride of life--is not of the Father but is of the world. And the world is passing away, and the lust of it; but he who does the will of God abides forever" (1 John 2:15-17).*

Everyone experiences temptation. No one is exempt. Even Jesus, when He was in the flesh, experienced temptation, but He did not sin (Hebrews 4:15).

Temptation is not sin. Being tempted is not sin, but yielding and acting upon it is sin.

One purpose of temptation is to glorify God. *"In this you greatly rejoice, though now for a little while you may have had to suffer grief in all kinds of trials. These have come so that your faith--of greater worth than gold, which perishes even though refined by fire--may be proved genuine and may result in praise, glory and honor when Jesus Christ is revealed" (1 Peter 1:7).*

There is always a way of escape. You do not have to yield to temptation.   In every temptation, God provides a way of escape (1 Corinthians 10:13).

DEALING WITH TEMPTATION:

If you have yielded to temptation, repent.   Temptation is sin only when it is acted upon. If you have sinned by acting upon temptation, you must repent (1 John 1:8-9).

Avoid places of temptation. Do not go places where you are tempted to sin. Be careful about what you hear and see, as the ear-gate and eye-gate are how temptation often gains access to your life. Do not associate with people who tend to lead you in to temptation.

Pray the daily prayer which appeals to God to "lead us not into temptation" (Matthew 6:13).

Reprogram your mind. Temptation starts with desire, then sin is conceived and birthed. Stop tempting thoughts the minute they enter your mind before sin is conceived and birthed. Rebuke the thoughts and tell them to go in the name of Jesus!

Read the Bible and pray. Prayer and Bible study are essential to living a life of victory over temptation. Jesus said to be prayerful, lest you enter into temptation (Matthew 26:41). David declared that he hid God's Word in his heart to keep him from sin (Psalm 119:11).

Meet temptation with the Word of God. Study the temptation of Jesus recorded in Matthew 4:1-11. He met every temptation with the Word of God. You can do likewise.

Use the escape hatch. The Bible says that in every temptation there is a way of escape (1 Corinthians 10:13). Look for the escape hatch and use it! Readjust your thoughts. Walk away from the errant group or the sinful pleasure. Remove yourself from temptation. Look for the way out, and take it! Escaping temptation may be immediate or a process, but there is always a way out.

WHAT GOD' WORD SAYS ABOUT TEMPTATION:

I have hidden your word in my heart that I might not sin against you. (Psalm 119:11)

Like a muddied spring or a polluted well is a righteous man who gives way to the wicked. (Proverbs 25:26)

And lead us not into temptation, but deliver us from the evil one. (Matthew 6:13)

Watch and pray so that you will not fall into temptation. The spirit is willing, but the body is weak. (Matthew 26:41)

And lead us not into temptation. (Luke 11:4)

When He came to the place, He said to them, "Pray that you may not enter into temptation." (Luke 22:40, NKJV)

Don't you know that when you offer yourselves to someone to obey him as slaves, you are slaves to the one whom you obey--whether you are slaves to sin, which leads to death, or to obedience, which leads to righteousness? But thanks be to God that, though you used to be slaves to sin, you wholeheartedly obeyed the form of teaching to which you were entrusted. You have been set free from sin and have become slaves to righteousness. (Romans 6:6-18)

For the power of the life-giving Spirit has freed you through Christ Jesus from the power of sin that leads to death. (Romans 8:2, TLB)

Therefore, I urge you, brothers, in view of God's mercy, to offer your bodies as living sacrifices, holy and pleasing to God--this is your spiritual act of worship. Do not conform any longer to the pattern of this world, but be transformed by the renewing of your mind. Then you will be able to test and approve what God's will is--his good, pleasing and perfect will. (Romans 12:1-2)

If you think you are standing firm, be careful that you don't fall! No temptation has seized you except what is common to man. And God is faithful; he will not let you be tempted beyond what you can bear. (1 Corinthians 10:12-13)

Do not be misled: "Bad company corrupts good character. (1 Corinthians 15:33)

You were taught, with regard to your former way of life, to put off your old self, which is being corrupted by its deceitful desires; 23 to be made new in the attitude of your minds; and to put on the new self, created to be like God in true righteousness and holiness. (Ephesians 4:22-24)

Put on the full armor of God so that you can take your stand against the devil's schemes. For our struggle is not against flesh and blood, but against the rulers, against the authorities, against the powers of this dark world and against the spiritual forces of evil in the heavenly realms. Therefore, put on the full armor of God, so that when the day of evil comes, you may be able to stand your ground, and after you have done everything, to stand, stand firm then, with the belt of truth buckled around your waist, with the breastplate of righteousness in place, and with your feet fitted with the readiness that comes from the gospel of peace. In addition to all this, take up the shield of faith, with which you can extinguish all the flaming arrows of the evil one. Take the helmet of salvation and the sword of the Spirit, which is the word of God. And pray in the Spirit on all occasions with all kinds of prayers and requests. (Ephesians 6:11-18)

Set your minds on things above, not on earthly things. For you died, and your life is now hidden with Christ in God. (Colossians 3:2-3)

Put to death, therefore, whatever belongs to your earthly nature: sexual immorality, impurity, lust, evil desires and greed, which is idolatry. (Colossians 3:5)

Yet the Lord is faithful, and He will strengthen [you] and set you on a firm foundation and guard you from the evil [one]. (2 Thessalonians 3:3, AMP)

Because he himself suffered when he was tempted, he is able to help those who are being tempted. (Hebrews 2:18)

For we do not have a high priest who is unable to sympathize with our weaknesses, but we have one who has been tempted in every way, just as we are--yet was without sin. Let us then approach the throne of grace with confidence, so that we may receive mercy and find grace to help us in our time of need. (Hebrews 4:15-16)

Flee the evil desires of youth, and pursue righteousness, faith, love and peace, along with those who call on the Lord out of a pure heart. (2 Timothy 2:22)

When tempted, no one should say, "God is tempting me." For God cannot be tempted by evil, nor does he tempt anyone; but each one is tempted when, by his own evil desire, he is dragged away and enticed. Then, after desire has conceived, it gives birth to sin; and sin, when it is full-grown, gives birth to death. (James 1:13-15)

Submit yourselves, then, to God. Resist the devil, and he will flee from you. (James 4:7)

In this you greatly rejoice, though now for a little while you may have had to suffer grief in all kinds of trials. These have come so that your faith--of greater worth than gold, which perishes even though refined by fire--may be proved genuine and may result in praise, glory and honor when Jesus Christ is revealed. (1 Peter 1:7)

Therefore, prepare your minds for action; be self-controlled; set your hope fully on the grace to be given you when Jesus Christ is revealed. As obedient children, do not conform to the evil desires you had when you lived in ignorance. But just as he who called you is holy, so be holy in all you do; for it is written: "Be holy, because I am holy." (1 Peter 1:13-16)

Be self-controlled and alert. Your enemy the devil prowls around like a roaring lion looking for someone to devour. Resist him, standing firm in the faith, because you know that your brothers throughout the world are undergoing the same kind of sufferings. And the God of all grace, who called you to his eternal glory in Christ, after you have suffered a little while, will himself restore you and make you strong, firm and steadfast. (1 Peter 5:8-10)

Now if [all these things are true, then be sure] the Lord knows how to rescue the godly out of temptations and trials, and how to keep the ungodly under chastisement until the day of judgment and doom, (2 Peter 2:9, AMP)

Do not love the world or the things in the world. If anyone loves the world, the love of the Father is not in him. For all that is in the world--the lust of the flesh, the lust of the eyes, and the pride of life--is not of the Father but is of the world. And the world is passing away, and the lust of it; but he who does the will of God abides forever. (1 John 2:15-17)

CHAPTER TEN

The "it" of Alcoholism

DEFINITION: An alcoholic is one who is unable to control drinking alcoholic substances, a person who is controlled by the desire, abuse, and misuse of alcohol. Their drinking is compulsive and out of control. Habitual use results in uncontrolled addiction.

FACTS ABOUT ALCHOLISM:

Alcohol can be addictive. Alcohol in the form of dinner wine is accepted in some cultures and is also used for medicinal purposes, but when used improperly it can become an addiction. When used in cooking, the alcoholic content is destroyed.

Wine in the Bible. The word "wine" in the Bible can mean either unfermented or fermented fruit of the vine. Priests were forbidden to drink wine (Leviticus 10:9) and kings were counseled not to drink it (Proverbs 31:4) --and we are called kings and priests unto God (Revelation 1:6). Jesus refused wine for medicinal purposes while on the cross (Mark 15:23), but drank of the cup at the Last Supper. The water that Jesus turned to wine could have been fermented or unfermented--we are not told. Personal conviction should be exercised in this area when wine is not an addictive issue.

You are not doomed for life. There is a slogan that says, "once an alcoholic, always an alcoholic" This statement is not true about a born-again believer who is a new creature in Christ. It does not mean that you cannot be delivered from alcoholism, but it does mean this is an area of temptation where you must continually be on guard. If you are or have been an alcoholic, you cannot drink ever again. Not even one drink!

Alcoholism can be passed down through families. Children of alcoholics tend to become alcoholics themselves--perhaps through learned behavior and/or generational spirits. This does not mean you can blame your alcoholism on your parents, however. You must take responsibility for your own addiction and deal with it so that you will not pass on this tendency to your own children.

Alcoholism is not a disease, it is a choice. If alcoholism is a disease it is the only one contracted by an act of the will; the only disease that is habit-forming; the only disease that promotes crime and brutality; and the only disease that is sold in a bottle in a store, and in some places, taxed by the government.

You are not alone. The temptation you are battling in regard to alcohol is common, but God has made a way of escape from it (1 Corinthians 10:13).

DEALING WITH ALCOHOLISM:

Recognize that alcohol abuse is a work of the flesh. It is listed among the works of the flesh (Galatians 5:19-21). It is not a sickness. The Holy Spirit can and will produce the self-control

52

needed to overcome this and other addictions as you allow the Fruit of the Spirit to be manifested in your life (Galatians 5:22-23).

Analyze why you need alcohol. Why do you need it? Are you trying to mask emotional pain? Do you rely on it to enable social interaction with others? If you determine why you drink, then you can deal with the root cause of your problem instead of turning to alcohol.

Admit that you need help. Proverbs 28:13 declares: *"He who conceals his sins does not prosper, but whoever confesses and renounces them finds mercy."* 1 John 1:8-9 gives both a warning and a promise: *"If we claim to be without sin, we deceive ourselves and the truth is not in us. If we confess our sins, he is faithful and just and will forgive us our sins and purify us from all unrighteousness."*

Ask God for deliverance. Pray not only about your alcoholism, but the root cause behind it--the loneliness, hurt, pain, inferiority, etc., that drives you to drink. Rebuke any generational spirits that would foster a desire for alcohol. Bind the spirit of alcoholism from operating in your life (Matthew 18:18).

Change your life-style. Do not attend events where drinking occurs and do not hang out with friends who drink. Do not watch television programs that promote drinking through either the screenplay or advertising. Do not return again to the bondage of alcoholism (Galatians 5:1).

Form a support network. Form a personal support network of people who have successfully recovered from alcoholism. Celebrate Recovery, Salvation Army, and Teen Challenge provide excellent Christian support network for addictions.

Remember that you never fail until you quit trying. If you start drinking again, don't give up in defeat. Ask God to forgive you and strengthen you to take control over your addiction through the power of the Holy Spirit. Then simply begin again. Rather than condemning yourself, think about ways you can escape the next time you are tempted. Understand that as a recovered alcoholic, you cannot take even one drink.

WHAT GOD'S WORD SAYS ABOUT ALCOHOLISM:

Wine is a mocker and beer a brawler; whoever is led astray by them is not wise. (Proverbs 20:1)

He who loves pleasure will become poor; whoever loves wine and oil will never be rich. (Proverbs 21:17)

Who has woe? Who has sorrow? Who has strife? Who has complaints? Who has needless bruises? Who has bloodshot eyes? Those who linger over wine, who go to sample bowls of mixed wine. Do not gaze at wine when it is red, when it sparkles in the cup, when it goes down smoothly! In the end it bites like a snake and poisons like a viper. Your eyes will see strange sights and your mind imagine confusing things. You will be like one sleeping on the high seas, lying on top of the rigging. "They hit me," you will say, "but I'm not hurt! They beat me, but I don't feel it! When will I wake up, so I can find another drink?" (Proverbs 23:29-35

Woe to those who rise early in the morning to run after their drinks, who stay up late at night till they are inflamed with wine. (Isaiah 5:11)
Woe to those who are heroes at drinking wine and champions at mixing drinks. (Isaiah 5:22)

Woe to him who gives drink to his neighbors, pouring it from the wineskin till they are drunk, so that he can gaze on their naked bodies. You will be filled with shame instead of glory. (Habakkuk 2:15-16)

Be careful, or your hearts will be weighed down with dissipation, drunkenness and the anxieties of life, and that day will close on you unexpectedly like a trap. (Luke 21:34)

Stand fast therefore in the liberty wherewith Christ hath made us free, and be not entangled again with the yoke of bondage ... For, brethren, ye have been called unto liberty; only use not liberty for an occasion to the flesh, but by love serve one another. (Galatians 5:1,13)

So, I say, live by the Spirit, and you will not gratify the desires of a sinful nature. For the sinful nature desires what is contrary to the Spirit, and the Spirit what is contrary to the sinful nature. (Galatians 5:16-17)

Do not get drunk on wine, which leads to debauchery. Instead, be filled with the Holy Spirit. (Ephesians 5:18)

For we do not have a high priest who is unable to sympathize with our weaknesses, but we have one who has been tempted in every way, just as we are--yet was without sin. Let us then approach the throne of grace with confidence, so that we may receive mercy and find grace to help us in our time of need. (Hebrews 4:15-16)

CHAPTER ELEVEN

The "it" of Eating Disorder

DEFINITION OF EATING DISORDERS: An eating disorder is an abnormal eating habit associated with deranged thoughts and negative feelings. Eating may be increased or decreased by binging or refusing to eat.

FACTS ABOUT EATING DISORDERS:

There are several types of eating disorders. Anorexia is when a person refuses to eat, expresses an intense fear of gaining weight, and becomes extremely underweight--sometimes to the point of starvation. An anorexic person sees themselves as "fat" no matter what their weight, and will often exercise excessively. Bulimia is characterized by binging and purging-- overeating and then forcing one's self to vomit afterwards. Binge-eating is overeating to the point of being physically uncomfortable--the biblical definition of this is gluttony.

Emotional issues are at the root of eating disorders. People who feel their world is out of control believe that eating is one area where they are in control. A sense of worthlessness, sadness, and depression may drive one to develop an eating disorder. A bad self-image--thinking one is fat and unattractive--also contributes to these types of problems. Stress, anxiety, rejection, guilt and shame are other emotions that trigger abnormal eating habits.

Eating disorders tend to develop during the teenage and young adult years, and they are more common in women.

There are no biblical restrictions on food for New Testament believers. The restrictions of the Old Testament were made under the law and were part of God's covenant with Israel. Some believers still choose to abide by these, but this is not mandatory according to scriptures and their beliefs should not be imposed on others. The New Testament clearly indicates that all things are pure (Romans 14:20-21) and believers are free to choose their diets (1 Corinthians 8:7-9). Paul warns about legalistic regulations: *"Since you died with Christ to the basic principles of this world, why, as though you still belonged to it, do you submit to its rules: 'Do not handle! Do not taste! Do not touch!'"? These are all destined to perish with use, because they are based on human commands and teachings. Such regulations indeed have an appearance of wisdom, with their self-imposed worship, their false humility and their harsh treatment of the body, but they lack any value in restraining sensual indulgence" (Colossians 2:20-23).*

Eating disorders lead to physical problems. Binging and purging through vomiting, diuretics, enemas, or laxatives can harm one's digestive tract. Being extremely overweight or underweight can affect internal organs, heart, blood pressure, and the functioning of the brain.

God does not want you to be in bondage to eating disorders or anything else. The Apostle Paul said: *"Everything is permissible for me but not everything is beneficial. Everything is permissible for me, but I will not be mastered by anything" (1 Corinthians 6:12).*

DEALING WITH EATING DISORDERS:

Admit your problem. Acknowledging that you have a problem is the first step in dealing with an eating disorder.

Determine the triggers that cause your problem. Identifying the issues that contribute to your eating disorder will help you deal with the root cause of it. Do you eat because you are lonely? Depressed? Because of stress?

Pray a prayer of deliverance. Ask God to deliver you from the bondage of eating disorders. Accept by faith, as you did your salvation, that it is done. In prayer, deal with any issues that contribute to your eating disorder. Ask God for deliverance from guilt, shame, depression, anxiety, etc. Ask Him to show you better ways to deal with loneliness, depression, and stress, etc. rather than eating.

Acknowledge that you have within you the power to change. You have the ability, through the power of the Holy Spirit, to put off old behaviors and put on new ones: *"You were taught, with regard to your former way of life, to put off your old self, which is being corrupted by its deceitful desires; to be made new in the attitude of your minds; and to put on the new self, created to be like God in true righteousness and holiness" (Ephesians 4:22-24).*

Surround yourself with supportive people. Recruit a few friends to provide prayer support. Get involved in a church or Bible study where you can receive additional support from other believers. If you know someone who has overcome an eating disorder, ask them to join your support team.

Learn to eat right. Learn what foods to eat in what amounts to develop a healthy lifestyle. A trained nutritionist can assist with this. No more binging and purging. No more dieting. No more fasting for losing weight. If you need to lose weight, develop a healthy lifestyle, exercise, and eat right.

Stick to a schedule. Have set times for eating and snacking. Set a schedule and stick to it. This will prevent you from becoming so hungry that you overeat.

Meditate on Scriptures that will help you overcome your disorder. The following is a list you can use for this purpose.

WHAT GOD'S WORD SAYS ABOUT EATING DISORDERS:

But the Lord said to Samuel, "Do not consider his appearance or his height, for I have rejected him. The Lord does not look at the things man looks at. Man looks at the outward appearance, but the Lord looks at the heart." (1 Samuel 16:7)

Nehemiah said, "Go and enjoy choice food and sweet drinks, and send some to those who have nothing prepared. This day is sacred to our Lord. Do not grieve, for the joy of the Lord is your strength." (Nehemiah 8:10)

Some became fools through their rebellious ways and suffered affliction because of their iniquities. They loathed all food and drew near the gates of death. Then they cried to the Lord in their trouble, and he saved them from their distress. He sent forth his word and healed them; he rescued them from the grave. (Psalm 107:17-20)

I praise you because I am fearfully and wonderfully made; your works are wonderful, I know that full well. My frame was not hidden from you when I was made in the secret place. When I was woven together in the depths of the earth, your eyes saw my unformed body. All the days ordained for me were written in your book before one of them came to be. (Psalm 139:14-16)

Charm is deceptive, and beauty is fleeting; but a woman who fears the Lord is to be praised. (Proverbs 31:30)

All beautiful you are, my darling; there is no flaw in you. (Song of Solomon 4:7)

So, do not fear, for I am with you; do not be dismayed, for I am your God. I will strengthen you and help you; I will uphold you with my righteous right hand. (Isaiah 41:10)

"For I know the plans I have for you," declares the Lord, "plans to prosper you and not to harm you, plans to give you hope and a future." (Jeremiah 29:11)

Therefore, I tell you, do not worry about your life, what you will eat or drink; or about your body, what you will wear. Is not life more important than food, and the body more important than clothes? (Matthew 6:25-26)

Watch and pray so that you will not fall into temptation. The spirit is willing, but the body is weak. (Mark 14:38)

Then Jesus said to his disciples: "Therefore I tell you, do not worry about your life, what you will eat; or about your body, what you will wear." (Luke 12:22)

Therefore, I urge you, brothers, in view of God's mercy, to offer your bodies as living sacrifices, holy and pleasing to God--this is your spiritual act of worship. Do not conform any longer to the pattern of this world, but be transformed by the renewing of your mind. Then you will be able to test and approve what God's will is--his good, pleasing and perfect will. (Romans 12:1-2)

Everything is permissible for me but not everything is beneficial. Everything is permissible for me, but I will not be mastered by anything. (1 Corinthians 6:12)

Do you not know that your body is a temple of the Holy Spirit, who is in you, whom you have received from God? You are not your own; you were bought at a price. Therefore, honor God with your body. (1 Corinthians 6:19-20)

No temptation has seized you except what is common to man. And God is faithful; he will not let you be tempted beyond what you can bear. But when you are tempted, he will also provide a way out so that you can stand up under it. (1 Corinthians 10:13)

So, whether you eat or drink or whatever you do, do it all for the glory of God. (1 Corinthians 10:31)

But he said to me, "My grace is sufficient for you, for my power is made perfect in weakness." Therefore, I will boast all the more gladly about my weaknesses, so that Christ's power may rest on me. That is why, for Christ's sake, I delight in weaknesses, in insults, in hardships, in persecutions, in difficulties. For when I am weak, then I am strong. (2 Corinthians 12:9-10)

It is for freedom that Christ has set us free. Stand firm, then, and do not let yourselves be burdened again by a yoke of slavery. (Galatians 5:1)

You have the ability to put off old behaviors and put on new ones: You were taught, with regard to your former way of life, to put off your old self, which is being corrupted by its deceitful desires; to be made new in the attitude of your minds; and to put on the new self, created to be like God in true righteousness and holiness. (Ephesians 4:22-24)

Put on the full armor of God so that you can take your stand against the devil's schemes. For our struggle is not against flesh and blood, but against the rulers, against the authorities, against the powers of this dark world and against the spiritual forces of evil in the heavenly realms. Therefore, put on the full armor of God, so that when the day of evil comes, you may be able to stand your ground, and after you have done everything, to stand. (Ephesians 6:11-13)

I can do everything through him who gives me strength. (Philippians 4:13)

Since you died with Christ to the basic principles of this world, why, as though you still belonged to it, do you submit to its rules: "Do not handle! Do not taste! Do not touch!"? These are all destined to perish with use, because they are based on human commands and teachings. Such regulations indeed have an appearance of wisdom, with their self-imposed worship, their false humility and their harsh treatment of the body, but they lack any value in restraining sensual indulgence. (Colossians 2:20-23)

Submit yourselves, then, to God. Resist the devil, and he will flee from you. (James 4:7)
Your beauty should not come from outward adornment, such as braided hair and the wearing of gold jewelry and fine clothes. Instead, it should be that of your inner self, the unfading beauty of a gentle and quiet spirit, which is of great worth in God's sight (1 Peter 3:

CHAPTER TWELVE

The "it" and God's Will, Guidance and Decision-Making

DEFINITION: In Greek there are two terms used for the word "will" in reference to the will of God. One word is "boulema," which refers to God's sovereign will. This is His predetermined plan for everything that happens in the universe. This type of "God's will" is fulfilled regardless of decisions made by man. The "boulema" will of God is written in His Word. There is no need to seek this will of God because it is revealed in the Bible. The other word "thelema" refers to God's desire for man to experience and live in His will. It refers to His individual plan for each believer. You have the power to choose whether or not you will walk in the "thelema" or individual will of God for your life. It is this "thelema" will, or God's will for you as an individual, to which we refer when we speak of seeking God's will.

FACTS ABOUT GOD'S WILL:

Seeking God's will for your life assumes several things. That you acknowledge there is a God, that He communicates with man, that you can recognize His voice, and that He has something to say. These are true according to the revelation in God's Word. It also assumes you have received Christ as Savior and are a believer (John 10:27).

Never seek guidance through the occult--witchcraft, tarot cards, tea leaves, fortune telling, horoscopes, etc. These are all satanic methods of guidance.

Do not use methods of chance to determine God's will. These include casting lots or fleeces. These methods were only used prior to the giving of the Holy Spirit in a new dimension where He came to live within believers (Acts 2). A fleece is only mentioned once in the Bible. It was used by Gideon at a time of great national crisis and was for confirmation of God's will, not for direction. Casting lots was a method similar to rolling dice to make a decision. These methods of guidance were never again mentioned after the giving of the Holy Spirit in Acts 2.

Every voice you hear is not God's voice. The Bible reveals that Satan speaks (Genesis 3). He lies, deceives, and attempts to lead you away from God. Satan even spoke to Jesus (Matthew 4:1-13). Evil spirits have voices (Acts 8:7; Luke 4:33-34). There is also the voice of self--examples of which are found in Luke 16:3 and 18:4 and in Jonah 4:8--and the voices of others who would give you advice. Then there is the voice of God, the voice that as a believer, you want to hear and follow.

God speaks through both the written and revealed Word. The first is called the "logos" Word of God. The second is called the "Rhema" word. The "logos" or written Word always agrees with the "rhema" or spoken, life-giving Word. A "rhema" Word from God usually applies to a specific situation, meets a personal need, and provides individual guidance. A "rhema" Word may be communicated through a sermon or a verse from the Bible which suddenly strikes you with great meaning. It may be spoken to you by God through the use of spiritual gifts. It may also be spoken in your inner spirit by the Lord. God will never guide you through a "rhema" personal word from God to do anything that conflicts with His written Word.

God reveals His will through the written Word of God, through counselors, through circumstances, and through open and closed doors of opportunity. God also gives supernatural guidance through angels, miracles, dreams, visions, or prophetic words spoken into your life. God sometimes speaks with an audible voice, but most often He communicates through a voice in your spirit. One of the most important ministries of the Holy Spirit is to guide believers into God's will: *"When He, the Spirit of truth is come (the Holy Spirit), He will guide you into all truth. . . and He will show you things to come and He shall receive of mine (God's will) and show it to you" (John 16:13-14, KJV).*

DEALING WITH GOD'S WILL:

Immerse yourself in the Word of God. Many questions regarding guidance are answered in God's Word. For example, the question of whether or not a believer should marry an unbeliever is addressed clearly in 1 Corinthians 6:14. There is no need to seek additional guidance or pray about something that is already revealed in God's Word.

Pray for God's will to be done. Jesus prayed: *"...yet not my will, but yours be done" (Luke 22:42).* Make this your prayer also. Ask God to teach you to do His will and to lead you by His Spirit (Psalm 143:10). If you do not know God's will in a certain situation, allow the Holy Spirit to pray through you because He intercedes according to the will of God (Romans 8:26).

Seek Godly counsel. Never go to a secular counselor, as they do not offer advice based on God's Word. As a believer, you cannot find God's purposes and plans for your life through advice from someone who does not know God and His Word (Proverbs 12:15).

Fulfill God's will for each day. If you obey the Word of God and His direction for each day, someday you will look back over your lifetime and realize you have walked in His will for a lifetime.

Expect God to open and close doors of opportunity. The Apostle Paul experienced both closed and open doors of opportunity--and so will you (1 Corinthians 16:9; Acts 16:6). Step through the open doors and stop at the closed doors, recognizing that closed doors are also used to direct your life. Never try to open a door that God has closed.

Trust God to guide you even when you do not understand. *"Trust in the Lord with all your heart and lean not on your own understanding; in all your ways acknowledge him, and he will make your paths straight" (Proverbs 3:5-6).*

Use the Biblical keys for guidance given in Proverbs 34:5-6 and Romans 12:1-2.

Remember that the individual will of God for you will never conflict with the moral will of God revealed in His Word.

Ask these questions when making decisions regarding questionable practices--things not mentioned in the Bible as being either right or wrong:

-Does it glorify God?
-What is your motivation for wanting to do this?
-Is it necessary?
-Does it promote spiritual growth?
-Is it an enslaving habit?
-Is it a compromise?
-Will it lead to temptation?
-Does it give the appearance of evil?
-Does it violate your conscience?
-How will it affect others?

Recognize that the peace of the Holy Spirit is your guide. For decisions not specifically dealt with by Biblical command, principle, for example, the peace of the Holy Spirit is your guide. When you make a decision regarding a questionable practice or life situation and you do not have peace in your spirit, continue to seek the Lord. Do not act until you have the peace of God confirming your choice.

Make wise decisions. Ask God for wisdom to make good decisions each day, and He will give it (James 1:5).

If you make a bad decision, do not give up in despair. Many people in the Bible strayed from the will of God but returned to fulfill their destinies: The prophet Jonah; the Apostle Peter; John Mark; and King David are some key examples. If this happens to you, admit your failure, repent, determine where you got off course, and correct your errors. Then seek God for new direction and act upon it.

Always remember that decisions determine destiny. Even your eternal destiny is determined by the decision you make regarding Jesus Christ.

WHAT GOD'S WORD SAYS ABOUT GOD'S WILL:

At the Lord's command they encamped, and at the Lord's command they set out. They obeyed the Lord's order, in accordance with his command through Moses. (Numbers 9:23)

Lead me, O Lord, in your righteousness because of my enemies-- make straight your way before me. (Psalm 5:8)

He guides the humble in what is right and teaches them his way. (Psalm 25:9)

Teach me your way, O Lord; lead me in a straight path because of my oppressors. (Psalm 27:11)

Since you are my rock and my fortress, for the sake of your name lead and guide me. (Psalm 31:3)

I will instruct you and teach you in the way you should go; I will counsel you and watch over you. (Psalm 32:8)

Commit your way to the Lord; trust in him and he will do this: (Psalm 37:5)

If the Lord delights in a man's way, he makes his steps firm; though he stumbles, he will not fall, for the Lord upholds him with his hand. (Psalm 37:23)

He lifted me out of the slimy pit, out of the mud and mire; he set my feet on a rock and gave me a firm place to stand. (Psalm 40:2)

I desire to do your will, O my God; your law is within my heart. (Psalm 40:8)

Send forth your light and your truth, let them guide me; let them bring me to your holy mountain, to the place where you dwell. (Psalm 43:3)

For this God is our God forever and ever; he will be our guide even to the end. (Psalm 48:14)

You will guide me with Your counsel, and afterward receive me to glory. (Psalm 73:24, NKJV)

Teach me your way, O Lord, and I will walk in your truth. (Psalm 86:11)

Your word is a lamp to my feet and a light for my path. (Psalm 119:105)

Direct my footsteps according to your word; let no sin rule over me. (Psalm 119:133)

Show me the way I should go, for to you I lift up my soul. (Psalm 143:8)

Teach me to do your will, for you are my God; may your good Spirit lead me on level ground. (Psalm 143:10)

Trust in the Lord with all your heart and lean not on your own understanding; in all your ways acknowledge him, and he will make your paths straight. (Proverbs 3:5-6)

For lack of guidance a nation falls, but many advisers make victory sure. (Proverbs 11:14)

The way of a fool is right in his own eyes, but he who heeds counsel is wise. (Proverbs 12:15, NKJV)

Commit to the Lord whatever you do, and your plans will succeed. (Proverbs 16:3)

Every way of a man is right in his own eyes, But the Lord weighs the hearts. (Proverbs 21:2, NKJV)

Whether you turn to the right or to the left, your ears will hear a voice behind you, saying, "This is the way; walk in it." (Isaiah 30:21)

And I will bring the blind by a way that they knew not; I will lead them in paths that they have not known: I will make darkness light before them, and crooked things straight. These things will I do unto them, and not forsake them. (Isaiah 42:16)

The Lord will guide you always; he will satisfy your needs in a sun-scorched land and will strengthen your frame. You will be like a well-watered garden, like a spring whose waters never fail. (Isaiah 58:11)

I know, O Lord, that a man's life is not his own; it is not for man to direct his steps. (Jeremiah 10:23)

Your will be done on earth as it is in heaven. (Matthew 6:10)

Not everyone who says to me, "Lord, Lord," will enter the kingdom of heaven, but only he who does the will of my Father who is in heaven. (Matthew 7:21)

Who are my mother and my brothers? he asked. Then he looked at those seated in a circle around him and said, here are my mother and my brothers! Whoever does God's will is my brother and sister and mother. (Mark 3:33-35)

Father, if you are willing, take this cup from me; yet not my will, but yours be done. (Luke 22:42)

For I have come down from heaven not to do my will but to do the will of him who sent me. (John 6:38)

If anyone chooses to do God's will, he will find out whether my teaching comes from God or whether I speak on my own. (John 7:17)

My sheep listen to my voice; I know them, and they follow me. I give them eternal life, and they shall never perish; no one can snatch them out of my hand. (John 10:27-28)

When He, the Spirit of truth is come (the Holy Spirit), He will guide you into all truth. . . and He will show you things to come and He shall receive of mine (God's will) and show it to you. (John 16:13-14, KJV)

In the same way, the Spirit helps us in our weakness. We do not know what we ought to pray for, but the Spirit himself intercedes for us with groans that words cannot express. And he who searches our hearts knows the mind of the Spirit, because the Spirit intercedes for the saints in accordance with God's will. (Romans 8:26-27)

Therefore, I urge you, brothers, in view of God's mercy, to offer your bodies as living sacrifices, holy and pleasing to God — this is your spiritual act of worship. Do not conform any longer to the pattern of this world, but be transformed by the renewing of your mind. Then you will be able to test and approve what God's will is his good, pleasing and perfect will. (Romans 12:1-2)

Since we live by the Spirit, let us keep in step with the Spirit. (Galatians 5:26)

And he made known to us the mystery of his will according to his good pleasure, which he purposed in Christ, to be put into effect when the times will have reached their fulfillment--to bring all things in heaven and on earth together under one head, even Christ. (Ephesians 1:9-10)

Therefore, do not be foolish, but understand what the Lord's will is. (Ephesians 5:17)

Continue to work out your salvation with fear and trembling, for it is God who works in you to will and to act according to his good purpose. (Philippians 2:12-13)

We have not stopped praying for you and asking God to fill you with the knowledge of his will through all spiritual wisdom and understanding. (Colossians 1:9)

Therefore, as the Holy Spirit says: "Today, if you will hear His voice, Do not harden your hearts as in the rebellion, In the day of trial in the wilderness, Where your fathers tested Me, tried Me, And saw My works forty years. Therefore, I was angry with that generation, And said, 'They always go astray in their heart, And they have not known My ways.' So, I swore in My wrath, 'They shall not enter My rest.'"   (Hebrews 3:7-1, NKJV)

You need to persevere so that when you have done the will of God, you will receive what he has promised. (Hebrews 10:36)

May the God of peace ... equip you with everything good for doing his will, and may he work in us what is pleasing to him, through Jesus Christ, to whom be glory for ever and ever. Amen. (Hebrews 13:20-21)

If any of you lacks wisdom, he should ask God, who gives generously to all without finding fault, and it will be given to him. But when he asks, he must believe and not doubt, because he who doubts is like a wave of the sea, blown and tossed by the wind. That man should not think he will receive anything from the Lord; he is a double-minded man, unstable in all he does. (James 1:5-8)

The world and its desires pass away, but the man who does the will of God lives forever. (1 John 2:17)

CONCLUSION

How to Get Rid of "it" though Personal Deliverance

When you understand self-deliverance, you will keep yourself from being bond; you will keep yourself healthy, physically and spiritually and be free from spiritual pollution. Every day, you will enjoy divine health and will not be spending your money on drugs and hospital bills.

Sometimes, there may not be a minister who is anointed and knowledgeable about deliverance to help you. Sometimes, you can be heavily attacked and the next service is about four days away. What do you do? You should never allow evil spirits to reside in your life. If you lack adequate time to do a self-deliverance in the mornings, after your quiet time, then, when you're having your bath, you could do it.

Whatever the causes of our spiritual afflictions, there are several proven steps we may try to help ourselves find freedom and healing. If these steps do not resolve your situation, then perhaps it is time to ask for help:

Step 1 — Conversion

Deliverance from any level of bondage, or harassment (collectively called, "spiritual afflictions") cannot be achieved without personal conversion. Deliverance from milder forms of spiritual affliction may often be achieved by the various acts of personal conversion—Acts of Contrition, Faith, Hope, Charity, and Consecration. "Prayer Acts" and other prayers, with fasting, and various devotions are often effective to drive evil spirits away:

So humble yourselves before God. Resist the Devil, and he will flee from you. Draw close to God, and God will draw close to you. — (James 4:7,8)

The first step, therefore, is make up your mind to live the Christ-life; or if already doing so, to persevere in living the Christ-life. This internal conversion, which is a conscious decision and determination to follow Christ and all of His teachings, precedes all other steps to deliverance. Without conversion to the Faith in Jesus Christ and participation in His family, the Church, deliverance, even if seemingly effective for a while, cannot be successful in the long run. It is the *"Truth"* that makes us free (John 8:31b), not prayers, rituals, counseling, or personal will in themselves. It is the confrontation with Truth that sends the demons running back to hell. This is why the method of Deliverance Counseling we use is called a *"Truth Encounter"*. As demons are confronted with the Truth, and as we are confronted with the Truth, of whom we are in Christ, we gain freedom. The foundation of all truth is Jesus Christ, who is Truth (John 14:6). Without our Lord Jesus Christ, we can never know truth or obtain it.

Some people believe they are unable to make a profession of faith in Jesus Christ. In such cases the person should ask God for help—ask Him for the faith that will save, deliver, and heal.

If we are willing to accept the gift of faith from God, our Lord will give it to us when we ask:

And I tell you, Ask, and it will be given you; seek, and you will find; knock, and it will be opened to you. For every one who asks receives, and he who seeks finds, and to him who knocks it will be opened. What father among you, if his son asks for a fish, will instead of a fish give him a serpent; or if he asks for an egg, will give him a scorpion? If you then, who are evil, know how to give good gifts to your children, how much more will the heavenly Father give the Holy Spirit to those who ask him! — (Luke 11:9-13)

Sincerely ask God for the faith that brings saving faith, the faith of conversion to the One, that is Jesus Christ, whom who declares:

I am the way, and the truth, and the life; no one comes to the Father, but by me (John 14:6) .... Come to me, all who labor and are heavy laden, and I will give you rest (Matthew 11:28) .... I will not reject anyone who comes to me (John 6:37) .... [rather] take my yoke upon you, and learn from me; for I am gentle and lowly in heart, and you will find rest for your souls. For my yoke is easy, and my burden is light (Matt 11:29-30)

Step 2 — Repentance

Essential to growing closer to God in faith, devotion, and love is to repent of those behaviors, desires, beliefs, and ideas that are sinful. The definition of sin is much broader than most people imagine. A definition of sin:

Sin is an offense against reason, truth, and right conscience; it is a failure in genuine love for God and neighbor caused by a perverse attachment to certain goods. Its wounds the nature of man and injures human solidarity. It has been defined as "an utterance, a deed, or a desire contrary to the eternal law."

Sin is an offense against God: *"Against you, you alone, have I sinned, and done that which is evil in your sight"* (Ps 51:4). Sin sets itself against God's love for us and turns our hearts away from it. Like the first sin (of Adam and Eve), it is disobedience, a revolt against God through the will to become "like gods" (Gen 3:5), knowing and determining good and evil. Sin is thus "love of oneself even to contempt of God." In this proud self-exaltation, sin is diametrically opposed to the obedience of Jesus, which achieves our salvation (cf. Phil 2:6-9).

We must repent of our sin, but repentance involves more than merely "turning away" from sin. Repentance must also renounce all that opposes God and all that He finds sinful. This includes renouncing Satan and his ways, renouncing personal sins, and renouncing all that leads us to sin. Some of the common sins and situations that interfere with deliverance include: involvement in non-Christian activities like the occult; persistent situational sins such as living together without marriage or remarriage without annulment of previous marriages; maintaining improper or problematic friendships; illegal activities of any sort; and sins that have become habitual such as pornography, masturbation, fornication, gossip, lying, stealing, etc.

The three greatest stumbling blocks to deliverance is Pride, Rebellion, and Unforgiveness and all the things that go along with those three sins. Repentance of Pride, Rebellion, and Unforgiveness is required to even hope for deliverance. Repentance also includes the firm amendment to avoid sin, and the near occasion of sin, in the future. Repentance requires a *complete* turnaround of our lives, a becoming a *"new man"*, so that...

...you should put away the old self of your former way of life, corrupted through deceitful desires, and be renewed in the spirit of your minds, and put on the new self, created in God's way in righteousness and holiness of truth. Therefore, putting away falsehood, speak the truth, each one to his neighbor, for we are members one of another...(thus) do not leave room for the devil (Eph 4:22-25,26b)

Step 3 — Confession

With faith and contrition of heart, repentance of mind, firm purpose to avoid sin and that which leads us to sin, we must now confess our sins before our God who is a God of forgiveness and mercy. This is a critical step that we will discuss at length.

The manner of our confession differs, but within our respective traditions, confession is required:

If we confess our sins, he is faithful and just, and will forgive our sins and cleanse us from all unrighteousness. (1 John 1:9)

... if you confess with your mouth that Jesus is Lord and believe in your heart that God raised him from the dead, you will be saved. For one believes with the heart and so is justified, and one confesses with the mouth and so is saved. (Romans 10:9-10)

"Confess your sins to each other and pray for each other so that you may be healed. The earnest prayer of a righteous person has great power and wonderful results" (James 5:16).

This confidant maybe one's pastor or another minister, or a trusted friend. We must be careful when choosing an "accountability partner." Since we will be revealing very private and sensitive information about ourselves, it is critically important to trust whoever we choose as a confidant to be discreet and to keep absolutely confidential the information we tell them.

There is wisdom in presenting oneself to an "accountability partner." Personal accountability is upheld when we confess to another person whom may hold us accountable for our actions. Confessing our sins to one another is a powerful way to break the bonds of sin in our lives. It is much harder to confess our sins to one another than to simply say, *"Lord, forgive me"*. While God is forgiving, of course, it is the demands of personal accountability before another human being that brings our confession into grounded reality that strengthens our commitment to turn away from sin in the future.

Religious ministers, psychologists, counselors, and others including the Deliverance Counselors of agency, are also bound either by law, ethical codes, or contract with the client (or bound by any combination thereof) to keep private and confidential all that is revealed to them. In addition, those in the ministerial and helping professions are usually trained in the ethics, legalities, and culture of maintaining confidentiality. They are use to keeping private the personal information of their patients and clients. Friends, on the other hand, may not have such training and may not be use to the culture of confidentiality. Thus, if one's confidant is not a pastor, or at least a minister, psychologist, or counselor bound by law and/or ethical codes, take care to ensure the chosen confidant understands thoroughly that he must keep private all that he hears and may not discuss it with anyone, not even with his spouse.

There is a great psychological comfort in hearing the words, "I forgive you" or the equivalent, "I absolve you of your sins." Our Father in heaven understands this psychological need. Thus, in His great love for us, He provided a way for us to hear those words in His name. It is God who ultimately forgives sins, but God, according to His sovereign authority chose to delegate this authority to His validly ordained priests. This power was given to the Apostles in John 20:22-23 and was passed on from them to those whom they appointed.

Our Father in heaven also knows and understands our need to be a family and for the family to come to our aid when we are hurting, to offer forgiveness when we fall, and to provide healing and strength to help us grow in faith. God forgives you when you appeal to Him with your heart-felt and sincere repentance and confession. Follow the tradition of your denomination and always offer a prayer for forgiveness as soon as possible after sinning. Then, in obedience to the Bible, seek accountability by confession to a confidant to complete your healing.

Step 4 — Removing the Greatest Stumbling blocks: Pride, Rebellion, and Forgiveness

We have already mentioned that the three biggest stumbling blocks to deliverance is usually Pride, Rebellion, and Unforgiveness. These three sins distance us from God. To draw closer to God we need to give up our pride, obey our Lord's teachings, and forgive those who hurt us.

In Deliverance Counseling we help our clients through exercises to locate pockets of pride and rebellion and to rid themselves of these sins with the help of God through prayer. Forgiveness, however, tends to be the most difficult, partly because of pride or even rebellion perhaps, but mostly because of deeply emotional issues surrounding the circumstances of the hurts someone has given us. Whatever the causes of our unforgiveness, deliverance is not possible until we can come to forgive, thus we shall discuss this topic at some length too.

The following guide is rather long, but this step is one of the most important. One simple MUST deals with Pride, Rebellion, and Unforgiveness if deliverance and healing is to be permanently possible.

Pride: Pride is the essential sin that leads to most other sins. It is the sin of Lucifer that led him to rebel against God resulting in his expulsion from heaven and becoming Satan.

Pride is a killer. Pride says, "I can do it! I can get myself out of this mess without God and without anyone else's helped." No, we can't! We absolutely need God, and we desperately need each other.

Pride also says "I know the best and most efficient way and how dare others get in the way of that" or "How dare things not go my way" or "How dare some person or something get in the way of what I want to do." Impatience is a factor of pride. Other ways impatience reveals our pride is getting impatient when we cannot find our car keys, or when we are late to a meeting, or if someone is driving too slowly for us on the hi-way, or when the computer acts up and interrupts our train of thought.

Impatience is the sister to Pride because it is caused essentially by our desire to have things our own way, in our own time, and according to our own preferences.

Pride is also the engine behind egotism (thinking more of oneself than one ought) and behind false humility (putting oneself down to be less than what one actually is). Pride is the force behind resistance to lawful and appropriate authority — whether that authority is a parent, teacher, police officer, government, employer, or the Church.

Pride is the basis of thinking of oneself as better than others, being pompous, and having contempt toward one's neighbors, employers, other family members, or the Church and her ministers.

Pride can also rear its ugly head in more subtle ways such as reluctance to apologize when we need to apologize, demanding our rights merely because it is our right, being inappropriately unkind or rude, jealousy, being quick-tempered, moodiness, brooding over wrongs done by others to oneself, depression and despair, or demanding that we are right about something, when indeed we are right about the issue, even though the issue is unimportant or can be handled differently (this is a major phenomenon in marriages, families, and friendships — the phrase "We need to choose our battles" is an important remedy for this).

Other ways that Pride expresses itself include: by taking personal credit for gifts or possessions and thus refusing to acknowledge that we have what we have by God's Providence; glorying in our achievements as if they were not primary a result of God's grace and divine goodness; by minimizing one's defeats; by claiming qualities that are not actually possessed; magnifying the faults and defects of others or dwelling upon the defects and faults of others.

James 4:6-10 and 1 Peter 5:1-10 reveals that spiritual conflict follows pride.

Examine yourself for these and any other attributes of pride and then pray:

Dear Heavenly Father. You have said that pride goes before destruction and an arrogant spirit before stumbling (Prov. 16:18). I confess that I have not denied myself, picked up my cross daily, and followed You (Matt. 16:24). In so doing I have given ground to the enemy in my life. I have believed that I could be successful and live victoriously by my own strength and resources. I now confess that I have sinned against You by placing my will before You and by centering my life around self instead of You.

I now renounce the self-life and by so doing cancel all the ground that has been gained in my life by the enemies of the Lord Jesus Christ. I pray that You will guide me so that I will do nothing from selfishness or empty conceit, but with humility of mind that I will regard others as more important than myself (Phil. 2:3). Enable me through love to serve others and in honor prefer others (Rom. 12:10). Amen.

Rebellion: We often place our confidence in the flesh not only with the "I can do it myself" attitude but each time we assert our own opinions above the teachings of Christ. It is a pride and a rebellion to say, "I want to do it my way" or "I want to think the way I want" without regard to the ways God teaches us to go and to believe. This is an arrogance that not only can get us into major trouble but also forms a major vulnerability for demons to come into our life.

Rebelling against God and His authority gives Satan an opportunity to attack. As our commanding general, the Lord Jesus Christ says, *"Get into ranks and follow Me. I will not lead you into temptation, but I will deliver you from evil."*

The Bible teaches us that it is the will of God for us to be obedient to parents, to civil government, to the Church, and to the pastors who are over us. We have two biblical responsibilities in regard to these authority figures: 1) Pray for them; and 2) submit to them. The only time God permits us to disobey those in authority over us is when they require of us an act or acquiescence in ways that are contrary to Church Law, Natural Law, or Divine Law.

Being under authority is an act of faith; we are trusting God to work through His established lines of authority. The authority that God has ordained does not mean, however, that we are to submit to abuse from those authorities. In those cases where someone in authority over us is abusing us in any way, then we need to act in appropriate ways according to the situation — such as appeal to the state for protection and relief for civil or criminal issues; or appeal to Church authorities on some issue involving religion or our parish; or make appropriate decisions such as terminating an abusive relationship, etc. Whoever the authority, who is abusing, we need to pray for the offender and to forgive him; but we are not required to be a doormat or target of their abuse.

Some of the lines of authority mentioned in the Bible include:

- Church leaders (Hebrews 13:17; Matthew 18:15-18)
- Parents (Ephesians 6: 1-3; Exodus 20:12)
- Husbands (1 Peter 3:1-3; Ephesians 5:23-24)
- Employers (1 Peter 2:18-21)
- Civil Government (Romans 13:1-5; 1 Timothy 2:1-3; 1 Peter 2:13-16)

Examine yourself for any areas of rebellion (deliberate driving faster than the speed limit is rebellion, too, you know!) and then pray:

Dear Heavenly Father. You have said that rebellion is as the sin of witchcraft and insubordination is as iniquity and idolatry (1 Sam. 15.23). I know that in action and attitude I have sinned against You with a rebellious heart. I ask Your forgiveness for my rebellion and pray that by the shed blood of the Lord Jesus Christ, strengthened by intercession of the that all ground gained by evil spirits because of my rebelliousness be canceled and taken back. I pray that You will shed light on all my ways that I may know the full extent of my rebelliousness, and I now choose to adopt a submissive spirit and a servant's heart. Amen.

Unforgiveness: Jesus Himself discusses the seriousness of failing to forgive. He tells us that failure to forgive those who hurt us will result in our not being forgiven ourselves by God. *"Forgive us our trespasses (sins) as we forgive those who trespass (sin) against us"*. The *Our Father*, the Lord's Prayer, which most all of us know and pray, Jesus teaches us that God will be as forgiving to us as we are to others.

Indeed, how can we expect God to forgive us when we do not forgive our brothers? Consider the follow teachings from Holy Scripture:

If you forgive those who sin against you, your heavenly Father will forgive you. But if you refuse to forgive others, your Father will not forgive your sins (Matthew 6:14,15).

But when you are praying, first forgive anyone you are holding a grudge against, so that your Father in heaven will forgive your sins, too (Mark 11:25).

If you forgive others, you will be forgiven. (Luke 6:37b)

Forgiveness is not about emotions and feelings. You can still be hurting, angry and upset and still decide to forgive. Forgiveness involves a mental decision, a decision of will, an act of your free will, even though you may not "Feel it".

The true nature of forgiveness:

1. **Forgiveness is not forgetting:** People who try to forget find that cannot. It is an unfortunate quirk of the English language with the phrase, "Forgive and forget". In actuality this phrase does not mean to "forget" in the sense of not remembering what happened; of course, we will remember. God says He will "remember our sins no more" (Heb. 10: 17), but God, being omniscient, obviously cannot literally forget. "Remember no more" means that God will never use the past against us (Ps. 103:12).

   To forget is really "to let go". We need to *"let go and let God"*. We let go of the past, but more importantly we let go of the hurt. As long as we do not forgive, as long as we do not let go, we allow the offender of our wounds continue to hurt us.

2. **Forgiveness is a choice not a feeling:** Since God requires us to forgive, <u>it is something we can do</u>. God will NEVER ask us to do something that is impossible for us to do; that would be cruel and God is a loving God.

   Forgiveness, however, is difficult for us because it pulls against our feelings and emotional hurts. Forgiveness is not about forgetting our feelings or our emotional hurts. We often will not "feel" like forgiving, but we must forgive anyway. As the Lord Prayer teaches us, God forgives us "as we forgive others". But how can God require this of us when we have been hurt so badly?

   God does not expect your feelings and emotional hurts to be healed overnight. He knows and understands our feelings and our hurts. He is a compassionate God and will help us to heal over time, as we are able. What God expects of us is not an immediate emotional healing, but a decision of will to forgive, a decision of will to trust Him to take care of the offender and to heal us, a decision of will to ask God for, and to commit to, being healed of our wounds.

3. **Forgiveness is not letting the person off the hook:** Forgiving is about you letting go, but it is not letting the offender off the hook. He will still pay for what he did, either before the Law or before God or both.

   Forgiving is surely difficult for us because it pulls against our concept of justice. We want revenge for offenses suffered. But we are told never to take our own revenge (Rom. 12:9). Revenge does more damage to us than it punishes the offender. God's justice will prevail, no one can escape it. Never fear, those who hurt us will be held accountable, but we must let God deal with it. In order for God to deal with it, we need to let Him deal with it by letting go.

   "Why should I let them off the hook?" But doing that is precisely the problem — we are still hooked to them, still bound by our past when we do not forgive.

   To forgive does not mean letting the person off the hook; it means letting yourself off the hook.

4. **But you don't understand how much this person hurt me:** The problem is that when we do not forgive we, in essence, allow the person to still hurt us! The question is, "How do we stop the pain?" The answer is **to forgive!**

   It is important to understand that we do not forgive someone for their sake; we do it for our sake so we can be free. Our need to forgive is not an issue between the offender and us; it is between us and God.

5. **Forgiveness is agreeing to live with the consequences of another's sin:** Forgiveness is costly. We pay the price of the evil we forgive. We are going to live with those consequences whether we want to or not; our only choice is whether or not we will do so in the slavery of bitterness and unforgiveness or with the freedom of forgiveness.

   Jesus took the consequences of our sin upon Himself. All true forgiveness is substitution because no one really forgives without bearing the consequences of the other person's sin. God the Father *"made Him who knew no sin to be sin on our behalf, that we might become the righteousness of God in Him"* (2 Cor. 5:2 1).

   Where is the justice? We might ask. It is the Cross that makes forgiveness legally and morally right: *"For the death that He died, He died to sin, once for all"* (Rom. 6: 10). This doesn't mean that we tolerate sin. We must always stand against sin, but we must give the offender to God and get on with our life.

6. **How do we forgive from our heart?** First, we acknowledge the hurt and the hate. If our forgiveness does not visit the emotional core of our life, it will be incomplete. Many feel the pain of interpersonal offenses, but they will not

acknowledge it. Let God bring the pain to the surface so He can deal with it. This is where the healing takes place.

Do not wait to forgive until we feel like forgiving; we will never get there. Feelings take time to heal mostly <u>after</u> the choice to forgive is made and Satan has lost his place (Eph. 4:26, 27). Freedom is what will be gained, not a feeling.

7. **Summary of Points on Forgiveness:**
   - Forgiveness is necessary to have fellowship with God.
   - It is not forgetting.
   - It is a choice.
   - Letting the offender off <u>our</u> hook is what frees us.
   - The offender is not off God's hook.
   - God says, "Revenge is mine."
   - You must acknowledge the hurt and the hate.
   - Forgiveness means we are agreeing to live with the consequences of another's sin — which we have to do anyway.
   - The justice is in the cross.
   - Choice is between the slavery of bitterness or the freedom of forgiveness.
   - Forgiveness means not using the past against the offender.
   - Forgiveness <u>does not</u> mean tolerating the sin or abuse.
   - Why forgive? To stop the pain! As we live in unforgiveness the offender still hurts us!
   - The issue of forgiveness is between you and God only.
   - The act of forgiveness is for your sake, and for your freedom.

Think about the people in your life for whom you need to forgive, people to whom you hold bitterness, people who have hurt you or disappointed you in anyway, or for whom you hold any kind of grudge. Be sure to ALWAYS include your parents, siblings, spouse, and YOURSELF. There is always something to forgive in our families and in ourselves.

Record all the names you can think of on a sheet of paper and a brief note as to why you need to forgive them. If you do not remember names, list them by what you do remember, such as "the guy in sixth grade with the red hat". If you cannot remember why you need to forgive someone on your list that is okay; forgive them for whatever it was — God knows.

After preparing this list ask God to bring to your mind anyone you have forgotten. It is not unusual to forget, or to push aside from our conscious mind, incidents and even the names of people whom have hurt us. These hidden hurts and wounds need to be healed as well. Thus, ask God to bring to your mind any person you have forgotten for whom you need to forgive, for whom you hold a grudge against, for which you are bitter, for those who have hurt you, with the following prayer:

Father in heaven, please bring to my mind the names of any people for whom I have held bitterness towards, grudges against, or have not forgiven for the hurts they have caused me. Help me to remember all these hurts so that they may be offered to You, O Lord, and healed from my soul so that I may live the truly victorious Christ-life. Amen.

Add to your list the names of anyone God may bring to your mind.

Now it is time to pray...

The following prayer needs to be said for each person on the list for which you need to forgive. Do not go to the next person on the list until you are sure you have dealt with all the remembered pain.

As you pray, God may bring to your mind various offending people and experiences that has been totally forgotten. Allow God to do this even if it is painful. Remember this process of forgiveness is for your sake because God wants you to be free.

Remember also that by forgiving the offender we are not rationalizing or trying to explain the offender's behavior. Forgiveness deals with the victim's pain, your pain, not another's excuses. Positive feelings will follow in time; freeing you from the past is the critical issue now.

If you are willing to forgive for your sake, so that you can walk away from this webpage free in Christ, free from the past and from person who hurt you, pray the introductory prayer below and then pray the "Prayer to Forgive" for each person on your list:

Heavenly Father, I now ask for your help in forgiving all those people on my list. Although I am still hurt and angry with them, I know that they are your children and that you love them more than I can possibly know. For this reason, my God, I ask you to help me forgive them. I lay down all bitterness, resentment and hatred for this person and I freely choose to forgive them. Teach me to be more merciful, my God, and help me be always willing, just as you are always willing, to forgive those who sin against me. Amen."

Prayer to Forgive

Lord, I forgive _________________________________ for (specifically identify all offenses and painful memories).

May God heal you and bless you!

Step 5 — Know Who You Are in Christ!

In order to gain freedom, it is important to know who you are in Christ. Thus, you need to evaluate the concept you have of yourself, to acknowledge the truth about God and about yourself; about your relationship and ideas about God and about the manner of our lives.

We often deceive ourselves about our position in Christ and our relationship with Him. For example, we may say to ourselves: "This isn't going to work" or "I wish I could believe this but I can't" or perhaps even more direct deceptions or denials concerning the promises of God for His children. Areas of deception that we may have include:

1. **Self-Deception** (telling ourselves things that are not true)

- o   Listening to God's words but thinking we do not have to do it (Ja 1:22; 4:17)
- o   Thinking we have no sin or do not sin (1 Jn 1:8)
- o   Thinking that we are something when we are not (Gal 6:3)
- o   Believing that we will not reap what we sow (Gal 6:7)
- o   Thinking we are wise and sophisticated in the 21st century (1 Cor 3:18, 19)
- o   Believing that the unrighteous will reach heaven (1 Cor 6:9)
- o   Thinking we can associate with bad company and not be corrupted (1 Cor 15:33)

2. **Self-Defense** (defending ourselves instead of trusting Christ)
- o   Denial (conscious or subconscious)
- o   Fantasy (escape from the real world)
- o   Emotional insulation (withdraw to avoid rejection)
- o   Regression (reverting back to a less threatening time in the past)
- o   Displacement (taking out frustrations on others)
- o   Projection (blaming others or accusing others of things we ourselves have done)
- o   Rationalization (defending self though verbal excursion)

To counter these and other deceptions we tell ourselves we need to exercise faith. Faith is the response to Truth and believing the truth is a CHOICE (not a feeling). If we say, "I want to believe God, but I just can't," then we are deceiving ourselves. Of course, we can believe God. We know that God does not lie. Faith is something we DECIDE to do; it is not something we FEEL like doing. Believing the truth does not make it true; rather it is TRUE, therefore we believe it.

Examine yourself and how you may deceive yourself with "self-deceptions" and "Self-Defense" mechanisms. The pray the following prayer: ...

Prayer to Know the Truth:

Dear Heavenly Father. I know that You desire truth in the inner self and that facing this truth is the way of liberation (John 8:32). I acknowledge that I have been deceived by the father of lies (John 8:44) and that I have deceived myself (1 John 1:8). I pray in the name of the Lord Jesus Christ, and since by faith I have received You into my life and am now seated with Christ in the heavenliest (Eph 2:6), I ask you Father to command all deceiving spirits to depart from me. I now ask You to *"search me, O God, and know my heart: try me and know my anxious thoughts; and see if there be any hurtful way in me, and lead me in the everlasting way"* (Ps. 139:23, 24) In the name of Christ Jesus I pray. Amen.

Knowing the truth about oneself, overcoming self-deceptions and the mechanism of self-defense that hide who we really are, includes understanding our faith in Christ. It is by Christ that our lives have meaning and substance.

The following prayer is the substance of that faith:

Affirmations

I believe that I am a child of God (1 Jn. 3:1-3) and that I am seated with Christ in the heavenlies (Eph. 2:6). I believe that I was saved by the grace of God through faith that is a gift and not the result of my own efforts or merits (Eph 2:8).

I choose to be strong in the Lord and in the strength of His might (Eph 6:10). I put no confidence in the flesh (Phil 3:3) for the weapons of warfare are not of the flesh (2 Cor. 10:4). I put on the whole armor of God (Eph. 6:10-20), and I resolve to stand firm in my faith and to resist the evil one.

I believe that Jesus Christ has all authority in heaven and on earth (Matt 28:18) and that He is the head over all rule and authority (Col 2:10). I believe that Satan and his demons and wicked spirits are subject to the Lord Jesus Christ and therefore to me in Christ since I am a member of Christ's body (Eph 1:19-23).

I believe that apart from Christ I can do nothing (John 15:5) so I declare my dependence upon Him.

I choose to abide in Christ in order to bear much fruit and to glorify the Lord (Jn 15:8) and to accomplish the work of sanctification that Christ began in me through the Cross (James 2).

I believe that since I am a member go God's royal family I have the authority, in the name of Christ Jesus, to ask the Father to command the devil to leave my presence, as I obey the command to resist the devil (James 4:7).

I reject any counterfeit gifts or works of Satan and his minions in my life.

I believe that the truth will set me free (John 8:32) and that walking in the light is the only path of fellowship and freedom (1 John 1:7). Therefore, as a royal member of God's household, I stand against Satan's deceptions by affirming all the doctrines of the Faith and by taking every thought captive in obedience to Christ (2 Cor 10:5).

I declare that the Bible and the Church are the only authoritative standards for me (2 Tim 3:15, 16).

I choose to speak the truth in love (Eph 4:15).

I choose to present my body as an instrument of righteousness, a living and holy sacrifice, and thus I renew my mind daily by the living Word of God in order that I may prove that the will of God is good, acceptable, and perfect (Rom 6:13; 12:1, 2).

I ask my heavenly Father to fill me with His Holy Spirit (Eph 5:18), to lead me into all truth (John 16:13), and to empower my life that I may live above sin and not carry out the desires of the flesh (Gal 5:16). I crucify the flesh (Gal 5:24) and choose to walk by the Spirit.

In making all these affirmations, I renounce all selfish goals and choose the ultimate goal of love (1 Tim 1:5). I choose to obey the greatest commandment to love the Lord my God will all my heart, soul, and mind, and to love my neighbor as myself (Matt 22:37-39). Amen.

Step 6 — Worship, Pray, and Fast

Worship as a Church Family: One of Satan's favorite lies, apart from having us believe that he does not exist, or that he does exist and is more powerful than he truly is, is that since God is everywhere and we can worship Him anywhere and do not need the "community of believers ", the Church family.

Although it is true that God is everywhere and worshiping Him anywhere is wholesome and good, it is false to believe that the Church is unnecessary. Since the earliest days of Christianity, communities of believers gathered together on the *Lord's Day* (Sunday).

Scripture is very clear on the subject of Church attendance and on how our submission to its authority is not only good but required. The Church, its leaders and members, are the Mystical Body of Christ here on Earth. To disobey the teachings of the Church as it relates to faith and morals is to disobey the teachings of Christ. To not attend church is also disobedience to Christ.

Paul admonishes those who do not come to Church in Hebrews 10:19-25:

Therefore, brothers, since through the blood of Jesus we have confidence of entrance into the sanctuary by the new and living way he opened for us through the veil, that is, his flesh, and since we have "a great priest over the house of God," let us approach with a sincere heart and in absolute trust, with our hearts sprinkled clean from an evil conscience and our bodies washed in pure water. Let us hold unwaveringly to our confession that gives us hope, for he who made the promise is trustworthy. We must consider how to rouse one another to love and good works. We should not stay away from our assembly, as is the custom of some, but encourage one another, and this all the more as you see the day drawing near.

Hebrews 13:17

Obey your leaders and submit to them; for they are keeping watch over your souls, as men who will have to give account. Let them do this joyfully, and not sadly, for that would be of no advantage to you.

Worship and prayer together as a family, prayer meetings, adoration, and other corporate settings, and in the privacy of the family at home is critical in developing spiritual health for the family and each family member. Such family devotion forms the foundation for all that each family does away from home in the world of school, work, and society.

Prayer is so important both in the family context and individually. It is important not just because prayer is something a Christian ought to do, but because prayer is communication.

The more we depend on God, the closer He is to us and we are to Him. Aligning ourselves with God, communicating with Him at all times and in all situations and personal decisions will unite our hearts to His. A heart united to the Creator will overflow with graces and blessings.

Prayer and Spiritual Warfare: In addition, a healthy prayer life destroys strongholds that demons may have in our lives and in our hearts. Without prayer we cannot hope to be delivered from spiritual afflictions. It is no secret —prayer, worship, devotion, and living the Christ-Life in all that it entails is the formula not only for deliverance from spiritual afflictions, but for living the victorious life in Christ.

When dealing with spiritual afflictions, however, some special prayer considerations may be needed. Scripture states that there are certain demons that will only respond to prayer as well as fasting: *"But this kind does not go out except by prayer and fasting."* (Matthew 17:21). If fasting can defeat even the strongest of fallen angels, just how powerful is this sacrifice that we can make?

Spiritual warfare prayers are very effective in defeating the enemy and drawing our hearts closer to God.

Step 7 — Live the Faith and Remain Faithful

Along with all the advice and recommendations of the first six steps, our healing and deliverance cannot be complete unless we act upon our faith. Doing good works and charitable acts of love are a natural outflow of our faith and necessary to lead a good Christian life. It is not enough to believe. James asks and admonishes in James 2:19,20, 26:

Do you still think it's enough just to believe that there is one God? Well, even the demons believe this, and they tremble in terror! Fool! When will you ever learn that faith that does not result in good deeds is useless?

Just as the body is dead without a spirit, so also faith is dead without good deeds.

James calls a man a fool who does not act upon his faith in James 1:22-25:

Be doers of the word and not hearers only, deluding yourselves. For if anyone is a hearer of the Word and not a doer, he is like a man who looks at his own face in a mirror. He sees himself, then goes off and promptly forgets what he looks like. But the one who peers into the prefect law of freedom and perseveres, and is not a hearer who forgets but a doer who acts, such a one shall be blessed in what he does.

It is hard to live the Christ-Life, but we must try. We must not have a faith that is dead and useless. We must not be a fool and not practice our faith. We must, rather, live out our faith and persevere in the faith:

1 Corinthians 9:23-27

All this I do for the sake of the gospel, so that I too may have a share in it. Do you not know that the runners in the stadium all run in the race, but only one wins the prize? Run so as to win. Every athlete exercises discipline in every way. They do it to win a perishable crown, but we an imperishable one. Thus, I do not run aimlessly; I do not fight as if I were shadowboxing. No, I drive my body and train it, for fear that, after having preached to others, I myself should be disqualified.

Colossians 1:17-23

He is before all things, and in him all things hold together. He is the head of the body, the church. He is the beginning, the firstborn from the dead, that in all things he himself might be preeminent. For in him all the fullness was pleased to dwell, and through him to reconcile all things for him, making peace by the blood of his cross (through him), whether those on earth or those in heaven.

And you who once were alienated and hostile in mind because of evil deeds he has now reconciled in his fleshly body through his death, to present you holy, without blemish, and irreproachable before him, provided that you persevere in the faith, firmly grounded, stable, and not shifting from the hope of the gospel that you heard, which has been preached to every creature under heaven, of which I, Paul, am a minister.

And thus, let us be able to say, with St. Paul, in 2 Timothy 4:6-8

For I am already on the point of being sacrificed; the time of my departure has come. I have fought the good fight, I have finished the race, I have kept the faith. Henceforth there is laid up for me the crown of righteousness, which the Lord, the righteous judge, will award to me on that Day, and not only to me but also to all who have loved His appearing.

Persevere in the faith and let your life be a living Gospel for you shall thereby *"know the truth and the truth shall set you free"*

I have outlined steps detailing certain issues that we have found important in gaining freedom for a person in spiritual affliction.

1. purify one's conscience by a good confession;
2. Receive Holy Communion as often as possible;
3. Implore the mercy of God by prayer and fasting.
4. Recourse to specific spiritual warfare prayers applicable to the situation.

Final Thoughts

Repentance, forgiveness, acting on our faith, praying, fasting, receiving the Sacrament frequently, and all the rest we ought to do as good Christians are very good things and very necessary for this life, but more importantly for the life to come.

The advice contained in these Steps to Self-Deliverance, however, are not "quick fixes". This advice involves a lifelong commitment for anyone with spiritual afflictions. Freeing yourself from the bondages of the enemy and keeping them from returning requires this commitment to persevere in Christ and in the Christ-life.

There will be dry times. Your faith will be tested. Indeed, the demons may (and more than likely will) try to return. Scripture speaks of what demons do once they are cast out:

Now when the unclean spirit goes out of a man, it passes through waterless places seeking rest, and does not find it. Then it says, 'I will return to my house from which I came'; and when it comes, it finds it unoccupied, swept, and put in order. Then it goes and takes along with it seven other spirits more wicked than itself, and they go in and live there; and the last state of that man becomes worse than the first. (Matthew 12, 43-45).

Do not leave your house (heart) *"unoccupied, swept and put in order"*; rather be filled with the Holy Spirit.

We can never let down our guard. As a final instruction, remember the teaching of St. Paul in Ephesians 6:10-18. We do not go about our day without putting on our clothes. Do not go into the world with God's armor:

Finally, draw your strength from the Lord and from his mighty power. Put on the armor of God so that you may be able to stand firm against the tactics of the devil. For our struggle is not with flesh and blood but with the principalities, with the powers, with the world rulers of this present darkness, with the evil spirits in the heavens. Therefore, put on the armor of God that you may be able to resist on the evil day and, having done everything, to hold your ground. So, stand fast with your loins girded in truth, clothed with righteousness as a breastplate, and your feet shod in readiness for the gospel of peace. In all circumstances, hold faith as a shield, to quench all (the) flaming arrows of the evil one. And take the helmet of salvation and the sword of the Spirit, which is the word of God. With all prayer and supplication, pray at every opportunity in the Spirit. To that end, be watchful with all perseverance and supplication.

APENDEX 1
Steps for Self-Deliverance

The purpose of all this information is to enable you to do a self-deliverance at home for yourself. The process of self-deliverance is carried out in stages. Let's go through them one by one.

STEP ONE: Start with praise and worship. You can sing songs to praise God and to worship Him.

STEP TWO: Confess out loud Scriptures promising deliverance. Luke 10:19, Ephesians 1:7, Romans 16:20, Revelation 12:11, Colossians 2:14-15, Galatians 3:13-14, Psalms 91:3…*2 Timothy 4:18* says And the Lord shall deliver me from every evil work, and will preserve me unto His heavenly kingdom: to whom be glory forever and ever. Amen. You should memorize *2 Tim 4:18*.

STEP THREE: Break covenants and curses to destroy their legal hold. You pray a simple prayer like this: I break any curse or covenant working against me, in the name of Jesus. (Simple prayers)

STEP FOUR: Bind all the spirits associated with those covenants and curses like this: I bind all the spirits attached or connected to the curses and covenants I have just broken, in the name of Jesus.

STEP FIVE: Lay one hand on your head and pray, Holy Ghost, cover me from the top of my head to the sole of my feet, in the name of Jesus. Begin to mention every organ of your body; kidney, liver, intestine, blood, etc. You must not rush at this level. Lay your hands-on areas that the Spirit of God leads you to.

STEP SIX: Then begin to saturate yourself with the Blood of Jesus. You do this by saying: I plead the Blood of Jesus over me. This must continue until you have a release in your spirit to stop.

STEP SEVEN: It is now, that you can demand firmly, in the name of the Lord Jesus Christ, that any spirit that is not of God should leave you. You demand it forcefully like this: In the name of the Lord Jesus Christ, I come against all you hidden spirits and I bind your activities in my life. You can no longer hide below the surface because I now recognize what you have been doing; release me, in the name of Jesus.

(**If sickness is the problem, address it and say**) You spirit of infirmity, I speak to you directly, get out of my life now. I am redeemed by the Blood of Jesus Christ, come out and go now. Go out with every breath by the power of the Holy Spirit. I prevail over you, in the name of Jesus.

STEP EIGHT: Ask for a fresh in-filling of the Holy Spirit and close the session with praises. Self-deliverance keeps you from getting sick; it removes every evil seed of the enemy; it charges your body with fire. It uproots evil plantations and builds up your confidence. Every night before you go to bed, you must remember these two important prayer points.

1. Pray for cover with the Blood of Jesus. **_Revelation 12:11_** = And they overcame him by the Blood of the Lamb, and by the word of their testimony; and they loved not their lives unto the death.
2. Pray that the Angels of God should surround you. **_Psalms 34:7_** = The Angel of the Lord encampeth round about them that fear him, and delivereth them.

No matter how sleepy you are, make sure pray these two prayer points every night. There is no reason why self-deliverance should not be effective. However, if the person seeking deliverance is under stubborn demonic control or hereditary strongman and lacks sufficient faith or authority to defeat the oppressors or living in any known sin, the evil spirits will be hard to get rid of. right.

 One final word of caution. For a person to be delivered, he/she must want deliverance. Self-deliverance must not be done because of pride, shyness, the fear of possible public embarrassment, etc. Your motive for engaging in self-deliverance has to be pure.

REMEMBER: **_DELIVERANCE IS A PROCESS (((NOT A ONE-TIME EVENT)))_** AND THE LENGTH OF TIME IT TAKES DEPENDS ON SEVERAL THINGS;

1. The length of time the spirit has stayed inside a person
2. The strength and reinforcement of the spirit
3. The experience and degree of anointing upon those who are ministering the deliverance
4. The willingness of the person being delivered to be free
5. The knowledge of the Word of God and your level of hatred for sin
6. SELF-DISCIPLINE IS NECESSARY

Also, remember that bondage can be weak or strong. A weak hold can be broken quickly, whereas a stronghold may take a more time. You will not realize the strength of bondage until you faithfully and persistently work on it. You must remember that a foothold can graduate to a stronghold if left unaddressed. After this exercise, set aside some days (with fasting). DO NOT CONTINUE TO DO THE THINGS THAT CAUSED THE "it"! CHANGE YOUR HABITS TO AGREE WITH YOUR PRAYERS. AMEN.

Appendix 2

Exposing the Doors to Bondage

Part I: The bondage

1. When did this bondage start?

2. Was there any unusual things that took place (or you did) when this bondage started?

3. If this bondage started when you were a child: Do you have ancestors who have suffered from a similar kind of bondage?

4. What kind of bondage are you facing? (Fears, depression, voices in your mind, mental illness, physical illness, mental torment, spiritual torment, etc... Please be as detailed as possible.)

5. What are all the things that have impacted your life? (Parent's death, trauma, a certain situation that changed your life, anything that 'changed' you.)

Part II: Your ancestor's background

1. Do you have ancestors who have struggled with similar problems or bondages?

2. Did your bondage start as a child and appear to have no reason to be there?

3. Do you have siblings who suffer from similar bondages or oppression?

Part III: Soul ties

1. Have you been involved with extramarital sex? Are you attracted to an ex-lover? Is he or she a good/godly influence for you?

2. Have you been divorced?

3. Do you feel an unusual attraction to a past boyfriend, girlfriend or lover (who is obviously not right for you)?

4. Do you let anybody dominate, control, or make your choices you?

5. Have you ever formed a blood covenant with another person? (Blood brothers, etc.)

6. Have you ever made vows or agreements with somebody in effort to strengthen the relationship or commit yourself to each other?

7. Do you see any ungodly relationships in your past where gifts were exchanged? (Are you holding onto something that was given to you from somebody you had adultery with, etc.)

8. Have you ever had ungodly relations with any one?

9. Do you have any pictures in your possession of somebody whom you may have an ungodly soul tie with? (A picture of you with somebody you had an adultery with, etc.)

Part IV: Relationship with parents

1. What do you think of your parents?

2. How would you explain your childhood?

3. Where you close to your parents while growing up? If not, why?

4. How would you explain your relationship with your parents? Was it good, bad or very cold?

5. Did you feel rejection from your parents?

6. Was either of your parents overly passive or controlling?

7. Has either of your parents been divorced? Remarried? Are your parents divorced?

8. How would you describe your relationship with your siblings growing up?

Part V: Rejection and abuse

1. Were your parents married when you were conceived? Were you the right sex? Did your parents not want you, or want you to be different (gender, etc.) in any way? If so, explain.

2. Did you feel rejected as a child? As an adult? If so, by whom? Explain.

3. Did you face abuse? What kind (emotional, physical, sexual, etc.) and by whom?

4. Have you faced rejection from your peers, classmates, friends or those around you?

5. Have you ever been put down, belittled, or made fun of? If so, by whom? Explain.

6. If you have faced rejection or abuse, how did you respond? Do you feel you are still paying a price for it? If so, how?

7. How do you respond to rejection right now?

8. Do you reject yourself (self-rejection)? If so, why and in what ways?

Part VI: Unforgiveness or bitterness

1. Is there anybody you feel edgy around? (Don't like them, feel anything in your heart against them, etc.)

2. Do you have anything against anybody? In other words, is there anybody that you have a hard time demonstrating the love of Christ to?

3. Has anybody wronged you that you haven't forgiven from your heart (thoughts, feelings, emotions, etc.)?

4. How do your view your siblings, parents, coworkers, etc.? Do you have any hard feelings against them?

5. Do you make a habit of blaming yourself for everything? Do you obsess over your mistakes and feel unusually guilty for them?

6. Do you deeply regret things that you've done in your past? Could you kick yourself over something you've done in your past? If so, explain.

Part VII: Personality

1. Are you a very positive or negative person?

2. Do you feel confident in yourself? If so, why?

3. Do you have a low self-esteem? If so, why?

4. Are you domineering or controlling? If so, to whom, and in what ways? Why?

5. Are you an achiever? (A go-getter) If so, in what ways?

6. Do you feel that you are always right and that if everybody did everything your way, this world would be a better place to live?

7. How do you treat your children? Husband? Are you controlling, passive, etc.?

8. Do you like people to 'look at you' (as in receive attention)?

Part VIII: Emotional health

1. Do you strive to feel accepted? If so, how does this affect your lifestyle? By whom do you want to feel accepted?

2. Are you always stressed out? If so, why?

3. Do you feel hurt? If so, by whom/what and why?

4. Do you feel good about yourself? If not, why?

5. Do you feel depressed? If so, why? When did it start? Did your parents or grandparents struggle with depression? If so, then do you know when it started and why? Do you have siblings who are also struggling? Do you feel your depression is rational or irrational?

6. Do you struggle with fears? If so, what is it that you fear? (Fear of heights, dying, being hopeless, failure, never marrying, etc.)

7. Do you worry about things? What things do you worry about? Why?

8. Do you struggle with anger? Do you have a short temper?

9. Do you have any insecurity? If so, explain.

10. Do you feel any self-pity or feel sorry for yourself? Have you ever felt this? If so, why?

11. Do you find it easy to hate people? If so, over what kinds of things would a person have to do to make you hate them?

12. Do you have any irrational feelings? If so, what are they?

13. Do you feel like something is wrong with you?

14. Do you feel excessively guilty over anything? Is this a continual problem?

15. Are you very confused and forgetful? (Beyond the normal)

16. Are you aware of any emotional wounds that have affected you?

17. Have you ever been deeply embarrassed over something? What was it?

18. Have you been in or are currently experiencing very difficult (depressing) circumstances which may cause you to feel hopeless or depressed?

Part IX: Who are you in Christ? And how do you see God?

1. How do you explain your relationship with God?

2. Do you feel you aren't good enough to meet His standards?

3. Do you see Him as a loving father, or a dictator?

4. Do you believe that it's only by the Blood of Jesus that your sins are forgiven? Or do you feel you need to earn your forgiveness in any way?

5. Do you feel God's love in your life?

6. Do you feel like your sins are forgiven? Or do you feel guilty?

7. Do you feel excessively guilty in everyday life?

8. Do you feel that doing good things, you earn God's love and acceptance?

9. Do you feel that God is angry or upset with you?

Part X: Spoken curses, vows & oaths

1. Have you ever spoken something negative about yourself that has come to past? For example: "I'm sick and tired..." or "If I don't quit typing, I'm going to get arthritis!"

2. Has your parents, or those in authority over you spoken out a curse over you? For example: "You'll never amount to anything!" or "You'll never get out of debt" or "You're so dumb"

3. Have you ever made a vow out of anger? If so, what? For example: "I'll never let anybody push me around again!" or "I'm never going to be hurt again!"

4. Have you ever wished to die? Have you ever said it?

5. If you have made any vows or oaths, what are they?

Part XI: Relationships

1. Do you have many friends? What kind of people are they?

2. Do you have a hard time trying to meet new people or make friends?

3. Are you socially outgoing or shy? If so, why?

4. How would you define your relationship with your spouse?

Part XII: Sexuality

1. Have you ever had unholy sex? What kind? (Fornication, adultery, sodomy, with a child, etc.)

2. Have you struggled with lust, fantasy or unholy sexual thoughts? If so, what kind?

3. Have you been attracted to pornography?

4. Do you have homosexual thoughts and desires? If so, have you acted upon those feelings?

5. How do you feel about your sexuality? (Do you feel dirty about it, or do you feel it's a wonderful blessing that God's given you?)

6. Do you withhold sex from your spouse or are you fidgety? Do you enjoy a healthy relationship with your spouse sexually? How does he or she react?

7. Have you ever been raped or sexually abused?

8. Have you ever woke up and felt a sexual presence with you? There are demons that imitate male and female functions, and stimulate their host (a person) sexually (beyond the normal 'wet dream').

9. Do you struggle or have you struggled with masturbation?

10. Do you struggle or have you struggled with any other sexual related thoughts, desires, or bondages?

11. Is there anything sexually that you are ashamed of?

Part XIII: Addictions

1. Do you have any addictions? If so, what kind? (Drugs, alcohol, smoking, eating, sex, TV, etc.) When did they start?

2. Did anybody else in your family (siblings, ancestors, etc.) have a struggle with any addictions? If so, what? Who?

3. Have you ever had, or currently have any sort of obsession over anything? If so, what?

Part XIV: False religions

Examples of false religions: Buddhism, Hindu, Jehovah Witness, Mormonism, Christian Scientists, eastern religions, etc.

1. Have you ever been involved with any false religions? If so, why, when and how long? How do you feel about those beliefs now?

2. Have you ever been involved in any secret societies such as Freemasonry? If so, how deep were you involved?

Part XV: The occult

1. Have you ever shown interest in the occult? If so, in what ways? (Read up on it, dabbled in it, etc.)

2. Do you still feel drawn or attracted to the occult?

3. Have you had any interest in horror or thriller style movies or novels? Are you still attracted to these things?

4. Have you ever made a vow with the devil? If so, what?

5. Married Satan?

6. Worshipped a demon or Satan?

7. Have you ever put a curse or spell on somebody?

8. Are you aware of any curses or spells placed on you? If so, what? Who did it?

9. Dabbled with an Ouija board? If so, why?

10. Ever been a member of a coven (group of 13 witches)? Explain.

11. Communicated with the dead? Explain.

12. Told somebody's fortune or went to see a fortune teller? Explain.

13. Ever read your horoscope?

14. Watched or been involved in a séance? Explain.

15. Have you been involved or a victim of Satanic Ritual Abuse (SRA)? Explain.

16. Been baptized into a false religion or any other evil baptism? If so, what were you baptized into? When?

17. Have you ever had a spirit guide?

18. Have you ever been involved with meditation, yoga, karate, or related activities?

19. Were you or anybody in your family superstitious? If so, who?

20. Ever been involved in astral travel? (Out of body)

21. If you have made any vows or oaths, what are they? Were there any sacrifices or rituals that were accompanied with them?

22. Have you ever made a blood pact before? If so, with whom (including persons, demons and Satan) and for what purpose?

23. Have you ever partaken in automatic writing, automatic drawing or automatic painting?

24. Have you ever been involved in Yoga, transcendental meditation, or similar activities?

25. Have you ever sought healing from a spiritual source other than Jesus Christ? (New age healing, energy healing, etc.)

26. Any other involvement in the occult? Explain.

Part XVI: Un-confessed sins

1. Are there any un-confessed sins that you have not repented of? (Usually something you've done, that you know is wrong, but won't admit to it. An abortion, stealing, etc. are some examples.)

2. Is there anything you've been hiding inside that you haven't confessed?

3. Do you feel excessively guilty over something(s) you've done in the past? If so, what?

Part XVII: Cursed objects

1. Do you have any idols, occult rings, or anything that could hold evil spiritual value in your home? If so, what? Any objects that hold evil spiritual value must be destroyed.

2. Do you have any gifts saved from sinful relationships? If so, explain. For example, if a man gives a woman a personal gift during an adultery that needs to be sold or destroyed.

Part XVIII: Severe trauma, abuse & disassociation

1. Have you ever been exposed to extreme abuse or a traumatic experience? Did it have a drastic effect on your emotional or mental system? If so, what happen? How did it affect you?

2. Have you ever disassociated or been diagnosed with Dissociative Identity Disorder (DID) or Multiple Personality Disorder (MPD)?

3. Are you aware of any alters (other personalities) that you may have? (If so, tell me about them)

4. Do you have a memory gap where you cannot remember a certain time of your life?

5. Do you have false memories of things that really didn't take place?

6. Have you ever been in a car accident or other traumatic situation? Have you ever witnessed a tragedy in real life?

Part XIX: Weaknesses

1. Do you struggle with any habitual sins? If so, what? Do you want to break those bad habits?

2. Do you struggle with any weaknesses such as lust, anger, hate, etc.? If so, what? Do you know where they came from or how they got started? Do you want to break free from those weaknesses?

Part XX: Pregnancy issues

1. Have you ever said something along the lines of, "I will never have children"?

2. Have you ever had an abortion or attempted one?

3. Have you ever had incest or ungodly sexual relations with somebody related to you? (See Leviticus 20:19-21, as this can cause a curse to land upon you which needs to be broken)

Part XXI: Other things to look for

1. Have you ever tried drugs? If so, how much, and how did it affect you? Why did you try drugs?

2. Have you ever thought about or attempted suicide?

3. Do you have any physical or mental disabilities, diseases or illnesses? Explain.

4. Do you want, and are willing to be delivered? Are you willing to give up those demon spirits and maybe make some lifestyle changes in order to keep your deliverance?

5. Do you experience unusual confusion settle upon you as you try to pray and read the Bible?

6. What kind of music do you like? (Please list all styles of music you currently enjoy, and give examples in each category you list, such as some names of artists and songs)

7. Have you previously enjoyed hard rock, metal, acid, alternative, rap, new age, or any other kind of worldly music? (Please provide some examples of artists and songs from each genre (type/style) of music you list)

8. Have you had any nightmares or weird experiences at night while supposedly sleeping?

9. Have you ever been in a trance or had an out of body experience?

10. Have you ever noticed time slipped right out from under you? For example, you look at your watch and its 7:00pm, then you look again what seemed like 15 minutes later and its 2:00am. This is a sign of a trance.

11. Have you ever touched or kissed a dead body? If so, explain whom and why and what happened afterwards.

12. Do you feel that you somehow have to earn your forgiveness? Do you 'wonder' if your sins are truly forgiven -- all of them? Are you aware of any signs of legalism or religious spirits operating in your mind?

13. Do you have any physical infirmities, sickness or diseases? If so, please list them.

14. Are you on any medications? If so, please explain.

15. Are you entertained by movies or TV shows which glorify death, murder, pain or suffering of others? Please explain.

16. Have you ever had any other kind of weird encounter with the spiritual realm?

Use this information to expose the root cause of the "it".

REFERENCES

1. Gary R. Collins, *Christian Counseling: A Comprehensive Guide*, 3rd Addition, Revised and Updated, NavPress, Colorado Springs, Colorado. ISBN 1418503290
2. Beilby, J.K. & P.R. Eddy. *Understanding Spiritual Warfare: Four Views*. Grand Rapids, Michigan: Baker, 2012.
3. Boyd, G.A., *God at War: The Bible and Spiritual Conflict*. Downers Grove, Illinois: IVP, 1997.
4. Hiebert, P. "Spiritual Warfare and Worldview"
5. Stedman, R.C, *Spiritual Warfare: Winning the Daily Battle with Satan.* Portland, Oregon: Multnomah, 1975.
6. Pirolo, N., *Prepare for Battle: Basic Training in Spiritual Warfare*, San Diego, California: Emmaus Road, International, 1997.
7. Arnold, E. C., *3 Crucial Questions about Spiritual Warfare*, Grand Rapids, Michigan: Baker, 1997.l
8. Rita Bennett, You Can Be Emotionally Free, 1982 ISBN 978 0 88270 748 8
9. Rita Bennett, Emotionally Free, 1982, ISBN 0 86065 194 0 Publishers, PO Box 777,
10. Tonbridge, Kent TN 11 0ZS, England, 1997, reprinted 2004). ISBN 1-85240-110-9. (Available in the US through the Arsenal Bookstore, 11005 Voyager Parkway, Colorado Springs, CO 80921.)
11. John and Paula Sandford, Healing the Wounded Spirit (Victory House, 1985). ISBN 0-932081-14-2.
12. Norma Dearing, The Healing Touch (Chosen Books, 2002). ISBN 0-8007-9302-1. Charles Kraft, Deep Wounds, Deep Healing (Servant Pub., 1993). ISBN 0-89283-784-5.
13. Derek Prince, God's Remedy for Rejection (Whitaker House, 1993). ISBN 088368-864-6.
14. Francis and Judith MacNutt, Praying for Your Unborn Child (1989). ISBN 0-38523-2829. (Available from www.Christianhealingmin.org, 904-765-3332.)
15. Thomas Verney, MD, The Secret Life of the Unborn Child (Summit Books, 1981).
16. Anderson, Winning Spiritual Warfare 1990 ISBN 13: 978-0-89081-868-8 James
17. Friesen, Uncovering the Mystery of MPD, 1997 ISBN 1-56819-062-7
18. Diane Hawkins, Multiple Identities, 2009 ISBN 978-0-9708073-6-6,
19. Restoration in Christ Ministries, http://www.rcm-usa.org/index.htm
20. Francis MacNutt, Deliverance from Evil Spirits, 1995, 0-8007-9232-7, Chap 17, pp 223-235 (best introductory material)
21. Daniel Ryder, Breaking the Circle of SRA, 1992, 0-89638-258-3 (an excellent book by a Christian counselor)
22. Margaret Smith, Ritual Abuse, what it is, why it happens, how to help, 1993, 0-06-250214-X (in depth information about SRA and MPD)
23. The Christian Bible
24. The following associations focus on trauma and disassociation www.sidran.org, www.issd.org
25. Pentecost, J.D., *Your Adversary the Devil.* Grand Rapids, Michigan: Zondervan, 1969

Dr. Paulette Douglas truly epitomizes elegance in living a saved, sanctified and Holy life, set apart from the secular world! Dr. Douglas is an ordained minister with the Pentecostal Assemblies of the World, an anointed national and international Evangelist, teacher and preacher. Dr. Paulette Douglas is renowned for the ministry of exhortation to the Body of Christ through deliverance, inner healing, salvation and biblical counseling at seminars, prayer clinics, crusades and conferences. She has established three churches and assisted in establishing many other churches, ministries and colleges as she serves on the Body of Christ for Jesus. Dr. Douglas was baptized in the name of Jesus Christ and filled with the Holy Ghost in 1977. She was called to the ministry in 1981, taught bible study at Pacific Bell for nine years which established the Radiant Life in Christ Ministries. She was the founder and pastor of the Radiant Life in Christ Community Church in Baldwin Park, California for nearly four years. Dr. Douglas retired in 1996 with full benefits from AT&T after 26 years of service. God introduced Dr. Douglas to the LOVE and HERO of her life, Bishop Robert T. Douglas Sr. They were married, the ministries merged, and she became the First Lady of the Jacob's Ladder Family, the Women's Ministry Director, the Church Executive Administrator and the Dean of the California University of Theology. Dr. Robert and Paulette Douglas are the proud parents of three wonderful children, Shakinah, Robert Jr. and Sondra Imani. They are also blessed with two granddaughters, Demi and Rob'Ann (butter ball) four grandsons, Dylan, Dominick Terrell, the twins Canden and Caden. Seven Godchildren and twelve God -grandchildren. Dr. Douglas is a graduate from Fuller Theological Seminary, Pasadena, California, Pentecostal Bible College, Ministerial Training Institute of Inglewood, California and Aenon Bible College West Coast. She has a Bachelors degree in Biblical Studies, a Masters degree in Theology, a PhD in Theology, Administration and a PhD in Biblical Counseling. She has earned certificates from California Christian Leadership of Orange County in biblical counseling, Zoe Christian Leadership Training Institute, Church Growth International, Seoul Korea and School of World Missions and Evangelism, Los Angeles. Dr. Douglas is formerly the Dean/Professor of the Inglewood Ministerial Training Institute of Inglewood, the Inland Empire Ministerial Training Institute, the Tri-County Ministerial Training Institute (San Bernardino, Riverside and Los Angeles counties) and the Living Waters Bible College, Rialto California. Dr. Douglas is presently the Dean of Colleges and Professor for the California District Council Aenon Bible College and Institutes, the Jacob's Ladder California University of Theology and Aenon Bible Institute CDC Extension Campus in Inglewood, California and the American College Theological Seminary International University (ACTS). All schools are fully accredited institutions for pastors, evangelist, teachers and anyone who has the call of God on their lives for ministry. Dr. Douglas is currently the CDC International Missions President and the past Church/Extension/Evangelism/Altar Director for the California District Council of the Pentecostal Assemblies of the World, Inc. Past Evangelism President for the CHDC Area 2 and has worked with the PAW Evangelism Ministry for more than 35 years. Dr. Paulette Douglas is the published author of the book series "Get Rid of It before It Gets Rid of You". Self-Help Instructions on how to correct and receive deliverance in every area of your life. Dr. Douglas portrays tremendous strength and endurance in the Lord by jointly sharing the vision and love for God with Bishop Douglas. Her primary objective in life is to be that "Excellent Woman of God, walking in His Divine favor.

**Books and Recourses Compiled by
Dr. Paulette Douglas**

"How to Get Rid of "it", Before "it" Gets Rid of You" Series (12 Books on Self Deliverance)

Volume One- Healing and Deliverance from Addictions

Volume Two- Healing and Deliverance from Sexual Addictions

Volume Three- Healing and Deliverance from Personality Disorders

Volume Four- Healing and Deliverance from Negative Relationships

Volume Five- Healing and Deliverance Through Spiritual Warfare

Volume Six- Healing and Deliverance from Negatives Attitudes

Volume Seven- Healing and Deliverance from Success Hindrances

Volume Eight- Healing and Deliverance from Tormenting Emotions

Volume Nine- Healing and Deliverance from Spiritual Weakness

Volume Ten- Healing and Deliverance from Salvation Issues

Volume Eleven- Healing and Deliverance from Domestic Problems

Volume Twelve- Healing and Deliverance Through Biblical Counseling

How to Have an Anointed Altar Workers Ministry

How to Have an Effective Prayer and Fasting Life

How to Walk in Your Grace as the Wife of a Minister, Deacon, Pastor, or Bishop

How to be an Effective Life Coach